D0411522

SEVEN
DILEMMAS
IN
WORLD
RELIGIONS

▼ ▼ ▼

SEVEN DILEMMAS IN WORLD RELIGIONS

▼ ▼ ▼

G. Lynn Stephens
and
Gregory Pence

PARAGON HOUSE
New York

First edition, 1994

Published in the United States by

Paragon House
370 Lexington Avenue
New York, New York 10017
Copyright © 1994 by Paragon House

Library of Congress Cataloging-in-Publication Data

Stephens, Lynn G., 1949–
Seven dilemmas in world religions / Lynn G. Stephens and
Gregory Pence. — 1st ed.
p.   cm.
Includes index.
ISBN 1-55778-702-6 : $16.95
1. Religions.   I. Pence, Gregory, 1948–   .   II. Title.
BL80.2.S726   1994
291—dc20   94-12102
CIP

Manufactured in the United States of America

Contents

▼ ▼ ▼

Preface

▼ ▼ ▼

Our aim in this book is both to ask and to rigorously pursue, answers to a few questions about some of the world's major religions. Our approach combines two traditional methods of studying religion. Philosophy of religion usually abstracts the distinctive features of particular religions and focuses on questions common to different religious worldviews: Does God exist? If God exists, why is there so much evil in the world? Is there an afterlife? On the other hand, the comparative study of religions emphasizes the distinctive qualities of the various religions. It tries to understand each religion from the inside and to get us to appreciate distinctive differences. It directs us toward such questions as: Why do Christians believe that Jesus was both human and divine? What do Hindus mean when they say that Brahman is the only reality? How can Buddhists both deny that we have souls and believe that we will be reborn in other bodies after we die?

Philosophy of religion and comparative religion also differ in their approach to the kinds of questions they ask. The former tends to be argumentative. Philosophers of religion don't just ask questions; they also rigorously examine the various answers people give to their questions and then ask more questions. If you answer yes to the question, "Does God exist?", philosophers want to know on what evidence you base your answer, as well as what you mean by "God." Philosophers also want to know whether you have considered all the implications of saying that God exists.

Scholars of comparative religion tend to be more accepting and less judgmental. They might gently request that you further explain your answer, but they seldom challenge it directly or continue badgering you if you reply that the answer is a mystery of faith that transcends human understanding.

In this book, we apply the argumentative methods of philosophy of religion to the kinds of questions typically asked in comparative religion. Each chapter focuses on a question internal to each of the following religions: Judaism, Christianity, Islam, Hinduism, Buddhism, and Confucianism. Within each chapter, we rigorously investigate various answers to a central question. However, we do not challenge the central presuppositions of the particular religion under discussion. We do not demand that Christians prove that Jesus really lived or that Buddhists prove that we are really reincarnated. As in the comparative study of religion, we are more concerned with understanding religious worldviews than with trying to show that they are true or false. But we believe that you cannot really understand a religious belief without examining it and without working out its implications. Doing that requires persistent questioning and taking a hard look at possible answers.

Though we aim to be rigorous, this is an introductory book. We do not presuppose any specific knowledge of world religions or familiarity with philosophic methods. Readers inspired to pursue for themselves the questions we discuss will discover that there is a great deal more to be said about each question than we say in this book. We often gloss over subtle distinctions and neglect potentially important lines of argument. We prefer intellectually exciting interpretation to more tentative and carefully qualified ones. We do not apologize for these limitations. Philosophical inquiry has to start somewhere. Usually, it starts in the middle.

I

Judaism in a Hostile World

▼ ▼ ▼

The Threat of Hellenism

Jews have always seen themselves as a people set apart. In this chapter, we explore the dilemma created by Jewish separateness. We do so by focusing on one historical period when tensions about separateness ran very high inside Judaism. The period we choose is the Hellenistic era, when the values of the dominant Greek culture swept over the ancient land of the Hebrews and Israelites.

The structure of this chapter is like a circle. We commence by discussing the origins of the idea that the Jews are God's treasured people and examine what this notion entails. Then, in the bulk of the chapter, we examine some major contrasts between Greek culture (not Greek philosophy) and Jewish culture. While doing so, we raise some issues about a separate Jewish identity and threats to it from Hellenistic culture. Finally, we complete the circle by contrasting two ways of maintaining Jewish identity: the way of withdrawal of the Essenes and the way of accommodation of the rabbis. We conclude with some speculation about the dilemma caused by Jewish separateness in subsequent history—a dilemma which continues to this day in Judaism.[1]

---

[1] On April 27, 1994, *The New York Times* ran an article about the simmering tensions between secular and religious Jews in Israel. It concerned whether the Orthodox rabbinate there would continue to completely control marriage, circumcision, and burial. The Ashkenazic Chief Rabbi, Yisrael Meir Lau, emphasized that "unbroken religious tradition has preserved the

1

A CHOSEN PEOPLE

If any scholar of Judaism was asked, "What is the central philosophical idea of all Jewish religion?" there could be only two answers: the Jews as the Chosen People and the task of Jews to live under the moral law. As we shall soon see, these two are really the same.

The doctrine of election within Judaism holds that God, whom ancient Hebrews represented by the tetragram "YHWH," chose the Hebrews as a special people for the most important task in human history. According to one story, all the peoples of the world were offered this mission but only the Jews accepted. According to a more ironical version of the same story, the Jews accepted only because they didn't understand what was required.

And what was required? According to Genesis, YHWH entered into a covenant with the patriarch Abraham. YHWH offered to give the land of the Jordan Valley to Abraham and his descendants if they would do two things: honor him before all other gods and circumcise male babies on the eighth day of life. Certainly, a bargain.

Abraham's covenant and the stories of Genesis probably took place between 2000 and 1700 BCE. About 1300 BCE, the second great covenant occurred after Moses led the Israelites out of slavery in Egypt (out of their "Egyptian Captivity"). When YHWH called Moses up Mount Sinai to receive his commandments, the relationship between YHWH and the Israelites grew more complex.

In Egypt, the Israelites had strayed from worshipping YHWH and had developed loose morals. Even as Moses spoke with YHWH, according to Scripture, the Israelites were falling into temptation. So YHWH made stricter terms in this second covenant. Yes, he would protect the Israelites, and lead them back to the fertile land. Yes, they

---

Jewish people for centuries. 'It begins with changes in the ceremony, and ultimately leads to marriages that are not according to Jewish law. History has shown that if the family is not established on the basis of religious law, Jewish existence is in danger. The minute you introduce a nonreligious ceremony, you can lead to intermarriage and assimilation.' " In a similar controversy about a play in Israel featuring an atheistic Jewish butcher named Fleischer, the rabbis emphasized that Israel should not become "just another Mediterranean country." (*New York Times*, November 11, 1993).

would be the Chosen People, and yes, they would have a special place in history.

But because of their tendency to sin and go astray, the Israelites had to pledge to live according to the laws given to them by YHWH through Moses. The prophet Nathan also later interprets the Law of Moses to bind even kings. So after David has had Uriah killed to take Uriah's wife, Bathsheba, Nathan asks the king what he would do to a rich farmer who owned many sheep but took his poor neighbor's one lamb for a feast. When King David furiously demands that this "farmer" be brought forward for punishment, Nathan flails his arm and points his finger at the king, crying out, "Thou art the man!"

Nathan and David lived around 1000 BCE. Five hundred years later, the Jews were released from their second ("Babylonian") captivity by the Persian king Cyrus the Great, who let Jews return to Jerusalem. There the powerful scribe Ezra and King Nehemiah feared that the Jews were losing their identity: Hebrew was becoming a dead language to the vernacular of the time, Aramaic, and the cosmopolitan influences of Persia and Greece were seeping into the lives of Jewish youth.

So the king and his scribe instituted several changes to create a secure tradition in Judaism: they created the final redaction (editing) of the Tanak (Hebrew name for the Old Testament); they announced that the Jews had ancient covenants with YHWH mediated by Abraham and Moses; they decreed that Jews were bound to live by the laws of these covenants or suffer horrible consequences; and they announced that the Torah (the first five books of the Tanak) would henceforth be read throughout the year in Hebrew in the Temple of Solomon.

These commandments (symbolized by the "Ten" Commandments) included rules promoting fidelity in marriage, dietary purity, hospitality to strangers, and worship. The Jews over time accepted this Mosaic Covenant and prospered in the Jordanian Valley and along the Mediterranean Sea.

King Nehemiah and the scribe Ezra created a tradition for Jews that would preserve Jewish identity. In doing so, they became ethnic separatists. They required Jews to renounce Gentile wives (and many

Jews must have had such wives). They insisted that Jews keep the Sabbath holy and not work on it. Since Jews also had to be able to walk to places of worship on the Sabbath, this law throughout the centuries would keep observant Jews geographically together in tightly bound areas. In later European cities, they would live in ghettos.

To keep Judaism pure, interpretations of these laws sometimes went very far indeed. If Jews are special with special access to God because of their purity, everything must be done to maintain that purity. So Judaism sets up severe penalties for intermarriage with non-Jews. Children produced without the legality of an official marriage are bastards in the full force of that term: they cannot enter a synagogue, they cannot marry a Jew, they cannot inherit money legally, and in general, they can have no full life within traditional Jewish society.

This is a severe, even shocking, penalty. But it worked. Like the judge who frees the criminal to teach police a lesson about following proper procedures, Judaism punished children for the sins of their parents. Knowing that parents love their children and want the best for them, Judaism turned that powerful emotion into a force for maintaining both sex within marriage and marriage within the Jewish community.

Throughout the following centuries (indeed, throughout thousands of subsequent years), whenever bad things happened to Jews, their leaders had a reply: "Bad things happen to us because we do not purify our lives; because we do not live according to God's law; because we deserve punishment for our bad ways. We are the Chosen People, but as such, we are held to a much higher standard of moral purity than other peoples. As a result, when we fail, we are punished more. As a people, we suffer more to achieve more for all of mankind."

This idea obviously has philosophical problems because it excuses every bad thing as God's will while simultaneously, and somewhat contradictorily, blaming the victims for every bad thing that happens to them. But we are more concerned here with the underlying assumption that Jews have a special mission in history and that part of fulfilling that mission is to live according to the Mosaic Law, especially as it was interpreted to mean living in the old, pure ways as a people separate from the dominant culture.

The desire for a separate Jewish identity created a dilemma for those who wanted the best for Jews. On one hand, separation preserves the identity of Judaism and as such, its existence. If Jews assimilated so much as to alter the very identity of a Jew, everything important would be lost. On the other hand, to stay apart had great costs. It branded Jews as "Other" and fueled anti-Semitic feelings. It kept Jews out of positions of power in the dominant culture. And when favorable change occurred, it sometimes prevented religious Jews from taking advantage of it, for example, if change conflicted with not working on the Sabbath or eating business meals with strangers who served pork. If Jews fell in love with non-Jews, it meant they could not marry.

What was better? To be apart and survive? To assimilate and grow, perhaps freeing individual Jews to do anything they wanted? How much could Judaism accommodate the outside without becoming itself assimilated? These were the questions that were important to Jewish leaders during Hellenistic times.

GENERAL HISTORICAL BACKGROUND OF HELLENISTIC CENTURIES

The Hellenistic era ran for roughly three centuries before the time of Jesus. It began with the ascent to the Macedonian throne of Alexander the Great (336 BCE) and reached its height afterward in the various kingdoms created by his former generals, including that of his lifelong friend, Ptolemy, whose cultured empire covered Egypt and Palestine. Another of Alexander's generals, Seleucus, tore off Syria and other eastern territories for his kingdom.

Unlike Alexander, Ptolemy lived into his eighties and established a clear line of succession to his son, Ptolemy II. The Ptolemies governed Egypt and Palestine between 300 and 201 BCE, giving Palestine a rare peace for an entire century and cementing the spread of Greek

culture into Palestine. The Ptolemies' northern neighbor, the Seleucid empire, coveted Palestine, and in 201, its king, Antiochus III,
conquered the area.

Seleucid kings ruled Jerusalem uncomfortably for the next thirty-
four years, constantly fighting the recalcitrant majority of Jews in the
country. The rural Jews retained strong religious affiliation not only
with their monotheistic God, YHWH, but also with the idea that Jews
were chosen for a special mission. These ideas nicely fit into the
aspirations of nationalistic Jews.

Today we remember the Greeks for their abstract ideas about
philosophy, political freedom, and art, and it is natural to suppose that
awareness of these Greek ideas first spread through trade and diplo-
macy to peoples such as the Jews around the Mediterranean Sea.
Such a modern, peaceful picture of the spread of ideas through
communication and commerce was not what really happened. The
superiority of Greek ideas was first felt through the siege machine,
the huge warship, and the relentless organization of first Greek and
then Macedonian society toward military victory.

The Greeks had learned to use their minds to bend the world to
their yoke. They not only had successful armies, but also had an
elaborate system of preparation for future victories, of which the
training of adolescent boys in the gymnasium was an important part.
The Macedonian phalanx, a force of 256 men linked 16 across and 16
deep, showed the enemy its layered "teeth"—a half-dozen hedgehog
rows of 17-foot spears. Invincible against cavalry, one enemy general
confessed that "the Macedonian phalanx was the most formidable
and terrifying sight" that had ever met his eyes.[2]

Wherever Alexander conquered, including Palestine, he began a
program that struck at the very heart of religious Judaism. Embracing
the idea of a unified world with a dominant, unifying culture, he tried
to eradicate regional identities, religions, languages, and customs. He
wanted the next generation to see itself as Greek citizens of a Greek
world, to speak Greek, and to pursue Greek ideals, and to abandon
the parochial customs of ethnic backwaters.

[2] Roman general Lucius Aemilius Paulus, cited in Robert L. O'Connell, *Of Arms and Men: A History of War, Weapons, and Aggression* (New York: Oxford University Press, 1989), p. 52.

After a successful campaign, many soldiers remained in a defeated country because they were given free land and amnesty from taxes as a return for their service. These men constituted a reserve army that could be called in a crisis. As part of his program of universalization, Alexander undertook a deliberate policy of miscegenation for his officers, ordering them to take local wives and granting their concubines privileges of free women.

Although Greek values were largely imposed on the great masses of Jews, they also gained the real allegiance of some young Jews, especially among the sophisticated upper classes. The "Greek attitude" offered young Jews a nonsuperstitious, cosmopolitan view of life (one fairly close to some contemporary American attitudes). The Greek meritocratic administrative system allowed talented young Jewish men to rise to real power, especially in Egypt under the Ptolemies. Some Jews were also educated in the Greek system, which meant that they became Hellenized. Some of these hoped that all Jews might one day lose their regional and religious identifications, that is, their distinctive ethnic character, and become real Greeks.

GREEK IDEAS AND VALUES

One of the most important Greek ideas was of *physis* (nature), a unitary, natural order underlying the apparent chaos of mere appearances. Considering the vast ignorance of the time and the conflicting accounts of everything from gods to medicine, this foundational idea was a great insight. Its importance was immense to later science and to Western civilization.

Not only did the Greeks come to believe that an underlying order existed in *physis*, but they also believed it was accessible to reason when intelligent people systematically studied it:

When we speak of the Greek miracle as essentially this, we have in mind [the] Greeks' insistence on making human life and action a projection of the rational mind, disposing these according to its own principles of abstraction and logic: in Greek philosophy and science, in the athletic and dramatic contests, in the elaboration of Athenian democracy, in the Athenian tragedies, in the history of Thucydides, and so on. We also see in it the genius with which the Greeks at once cultivated and limited the irrational and ecstatic. The result was a civilization radically different from all others then, and capable of surviving as high culture even after the death of its original matrix, the free polis. In a sense the whole course of Western civilization has been the triumph of Greek reason.[3]

Pythagoras revealed the Greek attitude when he forced nature to reveal his theorem. (He was so impressed that he and his followers worshipped math and numbers as divine.)

But the Greek mentality was more than the limitation of the ecstatic by the rational. It was also an emphasis on the naturalistic over the spiritual. Despite leanings in Plato's philosophy toward another world, Aristotle's worldly approach was far more in tune with ordinary Greek culture. The son of a physician, Aristotle used logic and empirical observation to try to understand his world. By the end of the Hellenistic era, the pursuit of more efficient war technology— such as the torsion catapult, the tiered trieme warships, and the hundred-foot tall siege tower—had pushed such Greeks as Archimedes of Syracuse toward the beginnings of the real study of science.

In this tradition, one of the greatest libraries in the history of the world was created by the Ptolemies at Alexandria with an astonishing half million papyrus rolls. Next to it resided the Museum (home of the Muses), one of the greatest research and teaching institutions of the history of humankind, even greater than Plato's Academy or Aristotle's Lyceum. Hundreds of scholars, including Euclid and Archimedes, came to study at these two great institutions.[4] These two institutions exerted a powerful attraction on intelligent, urbane, young Jewish men, who sometimes went to Egypt to study or work as administrators. The biblical story of Joseph modeled many other

[3] Fernando Gonzalez-Reigosa and Howard Kaminsky, "Greek Homosexuality, Greek Narcissism, Greek Culture, The Invention of Apollo," *Psychohistory Review: Studies of Motivation in History and Culture* 17.2 (Winter 1989): 155.
[4] Wallace Matson, "Hellenistic Greece," *A New History of Philosophy* (San Diego, Ca.: Harcourt Brace Jovanovich, 1987), p. 149ff.

stories of the Jewish boy who went to serve a foreign ruler and who there rose to a high position.

The other great, symbolic institution of Hellenism was the *gymnasium*, a word literally meaning "nude exercise." The gymnasium was the center not only of such exercise but also of Greek power. It was—all rolled into one—the men's club, country club, and executive dining room of its day. Inside the gymnasium, the *agon* (contest) occurred, not only in such sports as wrestling and the javelin, but also occasionally in literary and musical events.

The ethos of these Greek schools and gymnasia was to instruct young men in how to wage war and how to rule. Like later finishing and preparatory schools, they aimed at producing young gentlemen who exhibited the aristocratic values suitable for the ruling class: self-confidence, honesty with one's equals, skepticism toward traditional religions, military ingenuity, bravery, and a sophisticated appreciation of physical pleasures. The latter included those of food and wine, athletic prowess, and enjoyment of many forms of sexuality, including male homosexuality.

The gymnasium followed the elementary school, and together these two institutions grounded Greek education. It was in such institutions where groups of young men were socialized and molded to Greek ideals of *phronesis* (practical judgment), physical beauty, and warfare. In a certain sense, it did not matter whether one was born Greek; what mattered was whether one was educated as a Greek. To be educated as a Greek was to be a Greek.[5] If the Greek phalanx was the vehicle for the physical imposition of Greek life, the gymnasium and elementary school were the cultural vehicles.

Such schools and gymnasia gave the minority Greek ruling class a base of power in foreign lands. They insured that Greek values would be imposed on the conquered peoples, not the other way round. Very young boys attended elementary schools between ages seven and fourteen, followed by about two years as *epheboi* ("ephebates") training intensely in the gymnasium, followed by a stage of young man hood, again centered on the gymnasium.

[5] At least, as a participant in the dominant culture. Citizenship still was required for full power and was not always given, e.g., it is not clear that the Jews of Alexandria were ever granted the citizenship that many desired.

Because of the nature of pederasty, Greek man-boy sexuality, the *epheboi* were highly idolized and pursued by older Greek men. These young men wore the *petasos*, a broad-brimmed felt hat, and exercised in the nude. The Greek infatuation with sexuality, in brothels and among boys, was not shared by the Jews. Greek influence was felt most in cities, where sophisticated sexuality flourished, but made little impact in the countryside, where the Greeks mocked the Jewish religious "bumpkins."

The gymnasium was obviously the flash point of the conflict of the two conflicting worldviews. The two ultimate sacrileges for a Jew were either to renounce God or to undo his circumcision. In the gymnasium, statutes of the Greek gods Hermes and Heracles were customarily erected, forcing Jews to at least pay lip service to pagan idols. Some young Jews underwent a painful operation called *epispasm* to undo the effects of circumcision and to be able to participate in public games like the Greek young men destined one day to rule.

Such a display of a young uncircumcised Jewish boy at a gymnasium symbolized the three greatest antagonisms between Jews and Greeks. First, there was the assumption of antireligious natural philosophy, with its emphasis on reason, mathematics, evidence, and open-minded inquiry. This naturalism was discussed in the gymnasium and grounded the mostly skeptical view toward the statutes of the Greek gods and the outright condescension toward any local god, such as YHWH. Second, the gymnasium's emphasis on the body, on nudity, and on competitive, quasi-military games involving the body contrasted with Jewish attitudes of the time toward the body. Finally, the implicit universalism of the games and the gymnastic education, in which anyone could compete and learn so long as they adopted the basic Greek values, struck at the heart of a Jewish identity based on a people set apart by God.

JEWISH AND GREEK ATTITUDES TO SEXUALITY

Within Alexander's "one world" program was an underside that had a darker view of sexuality. The Greek emphasis on this life and the perfection of the body encouraged a freewheeling attitude toward sex. Greek culture was famously homoerotic, and many famous Greeks preferred anal intercourse with young boys over sex with women.

Definitive studies by scholars such as Dover, Greenberg, Sussman, and Boswell paint a picture of wild, polymorphous sexuality in Hellenistic times, with powerful Greek males having sex with both females and young boys.[6] As the classicist Martha Nussbaum emphasizes, the important aspect of such sexuality was not the gender of the sex partner but who penetrated whom.[7] Powerful people had the right to penetrate; the conquered, vulnerable, and weak were penetrated. As such, sexual relations could be said to be equally about sexual satisfaction and about power.

Many of these sexual relations were not consensual. Slavery was ubiquitous in Hellenistic times, and slaves were at the sexual mercy of their masters. Prostitution of all kinds was equally rampant and simply accepted as a dominant, but ordinary, fact of life. Some religious temples, especially those of fertility goddesses, were practically brothels. Children had no legal or ethical protection whatsoever other than "natural" parental affection, and it was not uncommon for a parent to sell a young child of eight into lifelong slavery or prostitution.

From the perspective of a modern world that takes seriously the ideal of moral equality between humans, this form of sexuality is immoral. It is not without merit to claim that this moral judgment, that is, that sexual relations should not consist of a dominating and an exploited person, has its base in ancient Judaism.

Speculating on why ancient Judaism did this, the modern Jewish apologist Dennis Prager argues that:

Man's nature, undisciplined by values, will allow sex to dominate his life and the life of society. When Judaism demanded that all sexual

[6] David Greenberg, *The Construction of Homosexuality* (Chicago: University of Chicago Press, 1988); K. J. Dover, *Greek Homosexuality* (Cambridge, Mass.: Harvard University Press, 1978, 1989); Norman Sussman, "Sex and Sexuality in History," in *The Sexual Experience*, eds. Sadock, Kaplan, and Freedman (Williams and Wilkins, 1976); John Boswell, *Christianity, Social Tolerance, and Homosexuality* (Chicago, Ill.: University of Chicago Press, 1980).
[7] Martha Nussbaum, "The Bondage and Freedom of Eros," *Times Literary Supplement* (London), June 1–7, 1990.

activity be channeled into marriage, it changed the world. It is not overstated to say that the Torah's prohibition of non-marital sex made the creation of Western Civilization possible. Societies that did not place boundaries around sexuality were stymied in their development. The subsequent domination of the Western world can, to a significant extent, be attributed to the sexual revolution, initiated by Judaism and later carried forward by Christianity.

This revolution consisted of forcing the sexual genie into the marital bottle. It ensured that sex no longer dominated society, heightened male-female love and sexuality (and thereby almost alone created the possibility of love and eroticism within marriage), and began the arduous task of elevating the status of women.

It is probably impossible for us who live thousands of years after Judaism began this process to perceive the extent to which sex can dominate, and has dominated, life.

Throughout the ancient world, and up to the recent past in many parts of the world, sexuality infused virtually all of society.

Human sexuality, especially male sexuality, is polymorphous, or utterly wild (far more so than animal sexuality). . . .[8]

Many scholars would object to some of Prager's sweeping, unqualified conclusions; for example, Prager fails to emphasize the power imbalance inherent in Greek sexuality or that historical Judaism made the man powerful over the woman in the marriage bed. Nevertheless, there is some truth in what Prager asserts. Within the marriage bed, no real restrictions were placed on sex; and sex there was celebrated and encouraged. Moreover, Judaism did indeed steer sexuality away from homosexuality, prostitution, premarital sex, and extramarital sex.

JUDAISM IN THE HELLENISTIC ERA

Jewish education of the time contrasted sharply with Greek education. We have here a difference in what might be called the gentleman/warrior model of education and the scribe/priest model.

[8] Dennis Prager, "Judaism, Homosexuality, and Civilization," *Ultimate Issues* 6.2 (April–June 1990): 2.

Even before the fifth century BCE when Ezra and Nehemiah produced the final version of the Tanak, a small elite group of Jewish
scribes—almost always from the tribe of Levi, hence called
"Levites"—had remembered and written down the ancient stories,
hymns, and history. Some of these writings survived to be included in
the Tanak. These professional writers dated at least back to the
Egyptian Captivity and had realized then that people could make a
living by knowing how to read and write. Like other such groups in
ancient times, they had profited greatly from this rare skill.[9]

At the beginning of the Hellenistic era, the Jews had schools where
the elite scribes were trained (in the pre-Maccabean era, the Jews did
not have general schools to train children, as the Greeks did).[10] These
scribal schools could have chosen to teach Jews the best of the Greek
wisdom. But this pro-Greek method would have meant the death of
Judaism because its brightest youth would have gone over to Hellenism. Instead, Jewish education chose the mode of preserving the
ancient writings and traditions. So each society, Greek and Jewish,
used its schools to ensure its tradition. Where Hellenism looked to
the future, Judaism looked to its past.

Judaism at this time existed not only in Judea but also in diaspora
communities such as Alexandria and Rome. Judaism needed common
bonds to tie this far-flung community together as Jews, yet the very
institutions it created to do so turned it away from the dominant,
Hellenistic culture. As Richard Seltzer writes,

> Perhaps more than for any other reason, the diaspora survived and
> flourished because of the canonization of the Scriptures. By Hellenistic
> and early Roman times, the Scriptures had assumed their final form and
> became the basis for popular Jewish education. Through the Bible, the
> Jews retained a common identity as a people covenanted with God and
> obligated to fulfill his commandments. The Bible as interpreted by the
> Jews maintained Jewish monotheism in self-conscious distinction from

---

[9] Priestly and scribal classes were significant and distinct groups throughout the eastern Mediterranean as far back as Sumeria in 3000 BCE.

[10] "A Jewish educational system did not exist in the pre-Maccabean period. . . ." (Elias Bickerman, *The Jews in the Greek Age* [Cambridge, Mass.: Harvard University Press and Jewish Theological Seminary, 1988], p. 303).

other religion traditions, preserved the Jews from the natural assimila-
tory pressures of diaspora conditions, and drew a sharp line between
them and their neighbors.[11]

The great institutions of learning of the Alexandrian Library and the
Museum there could not have been created from Judaism during this
time. Its model of erudition and scholarship came not from the West
but from the tradition of Persia, Babylon, and Assyria. From there also
came the Persian model of rule of hereditary king and high priest,
which Alexander emulated (with its pomp and lavish attire) to the
chagrin of his soldiers, and which his generals continued.

It was inevitable that these two cultures would clash.

JASON AND THE MACCABEES

The flashpoint occurred with the Maccabees and the event known in
Hellenistic history as the "Maccabee rebellion." In this section, we
will discover why the Maccabees, who successfully ousted the Syrian
king Antiochus IV and restored the temple, are celebrated in the
Hanukkah ceremony, but nevertheless occupy an awkward place in
Jewish history. We will see why the Sadducees, who were Jews who
embraced Hellenism and wanted all Jews to be assimilated into
Greek culture, were referred to as "wicked" Jews by the Jewish
author in the famous passage of Maccabees 1:

> In those days went there out of Israel wicked men, who persuaded
> many, saying, Let us go and make a covenant with the heathen that are
> round about us: . . . whereupon they built a place of exercise at Jerusa-
> lem according to the customs of the heathen: And made themselves
> uncircumcised, and forsook the holy covenant, and joined themselves
> to the heathen, and were sold to do mischief. (1.11–19)[12]

[11] Richard M. Seltzer, *Jewish People, Jewish Thought: The Jewish Experience in History* (New York: MacMillan, 1980), p. 177.
[12] *The Dartmouth Bible*, Sentry edition, ed. R. Chamberlain and H. Feldman (Boston, Mass.: Houghton Mifflin, 1950), p. 740.

These assimilationist Jews were seen by the author of Maccabees as no different than Greek heathens. Indeed, they were worse, because, as Jews, they knew that building a gymnasium in Jerusalem was a sacrilege.

These important events are described in the Scriptural books of the Apocrypha. For many centuries, the Apocrypha was placed in Christian writings between the Old and New Testaments, including the King James Version of the Bible for two hundred years, but it was omitted in 1816 by the American Bible Society, and it has been omitted since from bibles used by Protestants. The Catholic Douay Bible still contains Maccabees 1 and 2.

The fight between Jewish Hellenists and traditional Jews began in 175 BCE, when the Jewish priest Jason, an agent of the Seleucid king Antiochus IV, attempted to bring separatist Jews into the Greek assimilationist program. Symbolically, Jason had already changed his name from the Jewish "Joshua" to the Greek "Jason."

Jason now attempted to change Judea from a temple state to a Hellenized colony, that is, from a place where all citizens focused on sacrifices to YHWH at the temple in Jerusalem to a place where citizens gave their allegiance to Greek ideals. Jason built a gymnasium and began Greek elementary schools where upper-class Jewish children were given Greek names, read the *Iliad* in Greek, and were molded toward the warrior-gentlemen virtues of Greek aristocrats. Maccabees 2 tells us:

> And to such a height did the passion for Greek fashion rise, and influx of foreign customs, thanks to the surpassing impiety of that Godless Jason—no high priest he!—that the priests were no longer interested in the services of the altar, but despising the sanctuary, and neglecting the sacrifices, they hurried to take part in the unlawful displays held in the palestra after the quoit-throwing had been announced—thus setting at naught what their fathers honored and esteeming the glories of the Greeks above all else. (4.13–15)

The great historian of Judaism and Hellenism, Martin Hengel, emphasizes that these "revolutionary innovations of Jason and his followers inevitably shook the Jewish temple state to its very foundations."[13]

Jason and the Greeks saw their problem as how to bring the Jews, especially those not in Jerusalem but on country farms, into a larger whole not of the Jews' own choosing. The Greeks and Macedonians had done this before with countless small city-states and kingdoms along the Mediterranean Sea. In one gigantic sweep, Jason tried to brush aside the distinctive, unique character of Judaism and make Jerusalem into another Alexandria. Following Alexander, he used force to accomplish what acculturation had previously failed to do.

Ultimately he failed, and why he did so is extremely complex. Indeed, one of the most interesting questions in history is why Judaism alone was able to resist Hellenization and preserve much of its unique identity when almost all other cultures around the Mediterranean did not. At best, we will only sketch possible answers in this chapter.

Jason's backer, Antiochus IV, had decided that the obstinacy of the Jews stemmed from their fanatical devotion to the God they claimed as their own, YHWH (also translated as "Yahweh" and later mistranslated in the King James Version as "Jehovah"). If the distinctive religion of the Jews fueled their anti-Hellenistic feelings, Antiochus reasoned, then Judaism must go. Ruling through Jason, Antiochus compelled Jews to eat pork, banned both circumcision and possession of the Torah, and set up a statue of Zeus inside the holy inner sanctum of the temple.

Antiochus underestimated the resistance of the Jews to foreign rule. For over a century, the Jews of Palestine had already been taxed almost to the point of slavery, first by the Ptolemies and then by the Seleucid kings, who had even stolen from the treasury of the temple in Jerusalem. A people with nothing to lose is ripe for revolt. An unjust despot who oppressed almost all Jews served to unite together Jews who otherwise might have been at each other's throats.

As for foreign religion, the Hellenized Greeks and the pro-Greek Jews underestimated the allegiance of traditional Jews to YHWH and

[13] Martin Hengel, *Judaism and Hellenism: Studies in Their Encounter in Palestine During the Early Hellenistic Period* (Philadelphia: Fortress Press, 1974), p. 75. The account of Judaism and Hellenism in this chapter acknowledges its debt to Hengel's impressive work.

the power of that allegiance when fused with nationalistic desires for economic and political independence. Alexander had pragmatically adapted his Greek gods to the local gods of the people he conquered and—being no great believer himself—saw no reason why the Jews couldn't call YHWH the name of the great Greek god, Zeus. Countless Egyptians and Persians had done the same before. But in the eyes of some Jews, they were being asked to worship another god before "the Lord God" and to break the First Commandment.

So this revolt of Jews against Greek values should not be defined only as a battle between Greeks and Jews because it was more importantly a battle between two kinds of Jews. As the great scholar of Judaism, Elias Bickerman, argues, the battle was just as much inside Judaism as between Judaism and Greek culture.[14] Many Hellenist Jews were already polytheists, hedging their bets and paying tribute at the altars of Astarte, Baal, and numerous local gods. For them, changing the names of the gods or adding new ones was no big deal. These people were Hellenized Jews who wanted to become Greek citizens. They had adopted the language, values, and education of the dominant Greek culture and now wanted full citizenship.

The others were the religious and "nationalistic" Jews who refused to change their ancestral religion and who resented any foreign rulers. Bickerman is disliked among some Jewish scholars because he concludes that it was the ancient Jews who were "exclusive and intolerant," not the Hellenists, who were ready to welcome YHWH into their pantheon of gods.[15] Of course, seeing YHWH as just another god cut out the heart of the central religious beliefs of Judaism: no more one God, no more covenant with his Chosen People, and if no covenant, no moral law to sanctify one's life.

Jewish separatists drew the line against further assimilation at several points: one was circumcision of male babies on the eighth day of life by a rabbi, another was not eating pork, and another was keeping the Sabbath holy. Yet another was the recognition of only

---

[14] Bickerman, op. cit. The account of Judaism and Hellenism in this chapter also acknowledges its debt to Bickerman's scholarship. For a dissenting view, see Elias Tcherikover, *Hellenistic Civilization and the Jews* (Atheneum, 1970).

[15] Bickerman, op. cit., p. 256.

YHWH as the true god and no other. Recognition of any other deity, or any human as a deity, betrayed YHWH. The most primordial deal between YHWH and the Jews had been simple: "Thou shalt have no other gods before me." This primordial covenant, as interpreted by leaders over time, required the Jews to resist to death any attempt to weaken this requirements. So the Greek god, or the Roman emperor Caligula later, could never be equated with YHWH and could never be worshipped as a god. Nor could any hint of compromise be accepted, such as by making a small, extra offering to another god, or by kissing the ring of the local lord as if he were semidivine.

Hence one of the most famous stories of the Talmud, that of Hannah and her seven sons, each of whom refused any obeisance to Antiochus as god. As the story goes, Antiochus ordered the eldest son to worship an idol in front of his mother, Hannah, and her six other sons. The eldest refused and was promptly slain. One by one, Hannah's other five sons refused and were slain until the Syrian despot came to her youngest. To him, Antiochus whispered a secret compromise: when Antiochus dropped his ring, the boy merely had to stoop, pick it up, and give it back to Antiochus. The witnesses would assume that the son had given up his faith and bowed, but in actuality the boy would only be returning a dropped ring to its owner. The clever Antiochus offered Hannah's youngest son a chance to claim that his intention was not blasphemous, even though his behavior would be taken that way. But the son refused. Soon after, Hannah committed suicide. In the Talmud, Hannah and her sons are paradigms of those Jews who died *al kiddush ha-Shem*—to sanctify God's name.

To resist such blasphemies and injustices, the Jewish leader Mattahias fought a successful guerrilla war in 175 BCE against Antiochus IV and his Jewish minions. The revolt began when this country priest refused to make sacrifice to a foreign god. The preceding years had seen the acute Hellenization of Jerusalem under Jason and his Jewish Hellenes, but this had only been successful among upper-class and urban Jews, not the illiterate masses in the countryside of Judea. Mattahias's son, Judah, was such a successful fighter that he was known as "the hammer," or "Maccabeus" (hence, "Maccabees"), and kicked the Syrians out of Jerusalem, restoring the desecrated temple.

The feast of Hanukkah celebrates the oil lamp that "miraculously" burned for eight days during the temple's rededication. All Jewish children are told this story. But they are not always told the rest of the story, which had far more importance for the Jews of the time who opposed Hellenism.

To achieve victory against Antiochus, traditional, anti-Hellenistic Jews had aligned with the Maccabees, pro-Hellenistic Jews who sought the wealth and kingship of Palestine. To win, almost all Jews had to unite to free their ancient lands from the northern invader from Syria, Antiochus. But religious Jews lived to regret their unholy alliance with the power-hungry Jews who wanted a Jewish version of a Greek *polis*. As Seltzer writes, "the achievements of the Hasmoneans propelled them in the direction of becoming typical Hellenistic monarchs. Alexander Janneus called himself king, employed Greek mercenaries in his army, and surrounded himself with an increasingly Hellenized court."[16]

In 142 BCE, the Maccabee ruler Simon proved far more pagan than the Romans or Seleucids would have been. His grandson Yannai became entranced with his military prowess and adopted the style of the orgy-banquet made famous by the Greeks and Romans. In one such event, King Yannai carried on while forcing eight hundred Pharisees to watch the execution of their wives and children before themselves being executed. Over a thousand years later, the Marranos were Jews living in Spain and were terribly persecuted; as one Jewish commentator says about King Yannai, "It was as if the descendants of the Marranos had later become the leaders of the Spanish Inquisition. The Maccabees' terrible moral and religious decline explains why there is almost no mention of them in the Talmud."[17]

Hengel concludes,

For by and large the events between 175 and 167 BC which began with the introduction of gymnasium education and ended with the "abomination of desolation" marked a unique and deep turning-point in the

---

[16] Ibid., p. 182.

[17] Joseph Teluskin, "Maccabees, Hasmoneans, Mattahias, and Judah Maccabee," *Handbook of Jewish Literacy* (New York: William Morrow, 1991), p. 117.

history of Palestinian Judaism during the Graeco-Roman period. Only in that brief space of about eleven years under the rule of Antiochus IV was Judaism in the acute danger of submitting to Hellenistic culture as the result of the assimilation furthered by a powerful aristocratic minority. This deep crisis, which led to the attempt—which was undertaken primarily by Jewish forces themselves—decisively altered the religious and spiritual face of Palestinian Judaism. The ground was laid for that polemical and legalistic accentuation of Jewish piety which characterizes it in the New Testament period.[18]

The point of the story to anti-Hellenists is somewhat controversial, but the most likely interpretation is this: once the strictures of the Jewish religion are abandoned, there will be an inevitable descent into the kind of barbarous behavior of General Yannai. When traditional, religious, anti-Hellenist Jews allied with nationalistic, Hellenistic Jews, it was a slippery slope down an unstoppable path to corrupt anarchy. In some matters, any accommodation with Hellenism would prove fatal to traditional Judaism. All the evils come together once religious identity is lost: promiscuity, military priorities over spiritual ones, rape, pederasty, slavery, orgies, drunkenness, murderous rampages, excessive military retaliation, speaking and thinking in Greek, and ultimately, the death of the temple and the Chosen People.

The lesson of the Maccabees embittered the Jews and might have led them to redouble their resistance to encroaching Hellenistic culture. Politically, traditional anti-Hellenistic Jews lost their great battle with Hellenism seventy years later when Roman rule began in Palestine in 67 BCE. A few years before that time, Herod the Great's father, Antipater, had led the Sadducees in a revolt against the traditional Jews. After losing several attempts to win the throne, Antipater invited Rome to settle these internal disputes of the Jews.

After the Roman legions entered Jerusalem's open gates under General Pompey, Rome stayed as ruler. In 66 CE, when the Jews first began to rebel in their Great Revolt, the Roman general Vespasian began the final Hellenization of Judea, starting Rome's heavy-handed

[18] Hengel, op. cit., p. 77.

response. Before the siege of Jerusalem was over, Vespasian became emperor, and his son Titus was left to finish the job in 70 CE. A small group of Zealots fled to the hilltop fortress of Masada near the Dead Sea, and Titus besieged them until they committed mass suicide in 73 CE. Titus also destroyed the great temple, the previous center of Jewish religion. When the Jews rebelled again under Bar Kochba in 132 CE, the Romans dispersed the defeated Jews around the Mediterranean Sea as refugees and slaves.

ETHNICITY OR UNIVERSALISM?

Between 70 CE and 135 CE, Judaism almost died. Over the previous five hundred years, Jews had voluntarily dispersed from their ancient lands:

> The armies of Egypt, Alexander, and the Seleucids all had Jewish regiments. Others had settled abroad in the course of trade. One of the greatest colonies of Jews was at Alexandria, where they had gathered from 300 BCE. The Alexandrian Jews were Greek-speaking ... and when Jesus was born there were probably more Jews there than in Jerusalem, and in Rome there may have been as many as 50,000.[19]

After the Romans destroyed the second temple in 70 CE, the Jews involuntarily were dispersed over the Mediterranean shores and throughout Europe. This diaspora created the danger that all Jews might be absorbed, like many other cultures before them, into the dominant cultures into which they immigrated. Especially because some literal-minded Jews took YHWH to live inside the temple and to be the territorial god of Judea and Israel, danger existed that without a temple and homeland, Judaism might vanish.

But Judaism did not die after the Roman dispersion. How then did it survive? During Hellenistic times, both assimilationists and nationalistic separatists (Zealots) had been defeated. What ways of survival were left?

---

[19] J. M. Roberts, *A History of the World* (New York: Knopf, 1976), p. 235.

One way was the way of withdrawal. This approach was adopted by the Essenes of the Qumran community, whose Dead Sea Scrolls have recently caused much controversy. The Essenes broke away from orthodox Judaism, attempting to regain the traditional values of Judaism. To do so, they retreated from the glitter of Jerusalem and went out into the edge of the barren Transjordan desert, where they hoped their separation and pure behavior would develop a deep spiritualism. The Essenes at Qumran believed that the world would end soon, and they lived under a siege mentality. In part what was besieging this community, and what they went to the desert to escape, was Hellenism.

We have mentioned previously that the mission of the Chosen People in history was to live according to the law. Such a life increasingly was interpreted to mean living in a pure way: "In their history the Jews discerned an unfolding pattern by which they were being refined in the fire for the Day of Judgment. A fundamental contribution of Jewry to Christianity would be its sense of itself as a people set apart, its eyes on things not of this world . . . working to redeem the world."[20]

But how to live in a pure way? Jewish prophets such as Ezra, Nathan, and Isaiah had emphasized long before the Babylonian Captivity that only if the Jewish people purified themselves could the goal of history be achieved. The Essenes took the notion of self-purification in Judaism to an extreme.

Their flight to the barren desert shows just how much traditional Jews felt threatened by the glittering culture of urbane Jerusalem, just a few miles over the mountains from their caves. From the Dead Sea Scrolls, we can see how they lived in extreme asceticism to escape the worldly culture encroaching on them. With an elaborate network of gutters, cisterns, and pipes, they used water to purify themselves several times a day—both physically and spiritually removing their contaminations.

The way of withdrawal of the Essenes did not ensure survival partly because its metaphysics was faulty (there came no cosmic

[20] Ibid., p. 236.

battle of Armageddon between the Sons of Light and the Sons of Darkness). Another reason is that sects that completely withdraw from the world to prepare for cosmic war tend to die out, for example, the Branch Davidians in Texas under David Koresh. When Bar Kochba led his armed Jewish revolt in 132 CE, the Jews were crushed once and for all by the Romans.

Another method was the way of accommodation. It also involved purification, but in a much different sense. When Vespasian was conquering the last vestiges of Jewish resistance, Rabbi Yohanan ben Zakkai struck a deal with the Roman general whereby a small band of Jewish scholars were allowed to leave Jerusalem and live in the small town of Yavneh south of Jerusalem. To exist, the rabbinical school chose to accommodate itself to the dominant, militaristic, Roman culture.

In Yavneh began the great movement of rabbinical Judaism, in which a way of living in the world was gradually defined by many great rabbis as constituting a pure life. In this movement, power devolved from priests living in a temple to "teachers" or rabbis living among people as religious scholars. Eventually, two great centers of rabbinical scholarship arose, one centered around Jerusalem, the other in Babylonia, where scribes and education based on the East flourished. Out of these two places came the great commentaries on the Torah, the Babylonian and Jerusalem Talmuds. "The ideological revolution wrought by the rabbis of this period has carried Judaism through the best part of two thousand years."[21]

In the dark times after the final dispersion in 132 CE when almost all Jews were forced to leave their ancestral lands, the rabbis were faced with a question that had been implicit in the previous, voluntary diaspora: if a Jew can no longer live in his ancient lands and worship YHWH in his temple, what is a Jew? Here the rabbis came to agree with the Essenes. Both freed YHWH from the confines of his temple and the territory of Judea, seeing his power as more universal and as coming to any Jew who lived in a pure way.

The problem was to define "a pure way" by withdrawing from the

---

[21] Brian Lancaster, *The Elements of Judaism* (Longmead, England: Elements Press, 1993), p. 117.

dominant culture yet while existing amid it. If life cannot be purified by geographic isolation, then some way must be found within the dominant culture to exist and remain separate. Eventually, rabbis such as the great Akiva taught that the way to sanctify a Jew's life—to fulfill a Jew's special mission in history—was a set of daily actions. Which actions? What many rabbis as a group evolved over centuries, especially through "court" decisions at Jerusalem and Babylonia— as much more than the typical religious rituals at the high points of life involving birth, marriage, prayer, and death.

What the rabbis evolved was a way of life, a kosher way, in which almost all the actions and nonactions of daily life were defined in pure and impure ways. As one scholar put it, with the temple and its priesthood gone, the rabbis made of every Jew a "priest," made his table his "altar," and made his house and neighborhood into his "Temple and courtyard."[22]

All these decisions and more became kosher behavior in ways of eating, dressing, worshipping, and living. (Kosher [*kashrut*] ways of eating did not originate, as commonly believed, as an ancient Jewish health code, but as a way of making holy the preparation of food.) Such an attitude deliberately turned its back on Hellenization and concurrently on modernization. In the first century CE, small groups of Jews at towns such as Yavneh in Palestine also attempted to live a pure life in the belief that if one small group of humans lived in absolute purity, they could accelerate the end of history.

CONCLUSION

We conclude that, although Hellenization and then Romanization increasingly affected the surface of Jewish life, it never penetrated its core. For example, in Roman cities many Jews continued to live as a group and apart, usually in order to be within walking distance of synagogues on the Sabbath day.[23] The way of withdrawal won. It preserved Judaism as a historical religion through the ages.

---

[22] Eugene B. Borowitz, "Judaism: An overview," *The Encyclopedia of Religion, vol. 8, ed. Mircea Eliade (New York: Mac Millan, 1988), p. 130.*
[23] R. Patai, "Jews and Hellenes," *The Jewish Mind* (New York: Scribner's, 1977), p. 61.

Much to the chagrin of pro-Hellenic Jews, Greeks and Romans always saw the Jews as an "other" people living apart. Other supports of Judaism included pilgrimages to Jerusalem by members of the diaspora, missionary work to wavering Jewish communities, and the use of the Talmudic centers of Babylon and Jerusalem as courts of law.

Daily practice to purify or sanctify Jewish life established the identity of Jews. It ensured the survival of Judaism through the anti-Semitism of centuries of inquisitions and life among Europe's ghettos, and finally through Hitler's attempted Final Solution. In modern times, it left it open to charges of being "ethnocentric" or fostering "race consciousness." It steered religious (especially what is today called "orthodox") Judaism away from practical compromises with the world and away from public, assimilationist education, turning it instead toward its own distant past.[24]

Within Israel today, both forces within Judaism struggle against each other. In the hills fifty miles inland from the coast, historical Jewish religion thrives in Jerusalem, and the quiet of the Sabbath there is similar to all orthodox Jewish quarters for centuries. But on the glittering coast where most Israelis live, and where many are agnostic or atheists, cities such as Tel Aviv seem bent on complete assimilation to the modern world. So instead of a center of orthodox Jewish religion inside a dominant, outer pagan culture, we have now in Israel a center of orthodox, Jewish religion inside a dominant, outer culture of secular Jews. If we have been successful in this chapter, the reader will appreciate how the tension between these two forces inside Judaism, and inside Israel, is a very ancient one.

---

[24] We are indebted for comments on this chapter to Frank Leavitt, Jakobovits Centre for Jewish Medical Ethics, an anonymous professor in the Department of Jewish Studies, and Shimon Glick, Dean of the Medical School, all of Ben Gurion University of the Negev, Israel.

2

Was Jesus a Great Moral Teacher?

▼ ▼ ▼

In this chapter we consider the dilemma that arises when people attempt to separate the moral teachings of Jesus from his theological views. We use a quotation from C. S. Lewis to set up the problem and then, in the bulk of the chapter, examine the actual sayings of Jesus in the Gospels about some important ethical matters. At the end, we reconsider Lewis' view and what is at stake in it.

MORAL TEACHINGS WITHOUT THEOLOGY?

Modern scholarship suggests that Jesus of Nazareth was born around 4 BCE and was crucified sometime during the procuratorship of Pontius Pilate, who held that office from 26 to 36 CE. The four Gospels—Matthew, Mark, Luke, and John—provide us with our only substantive record of how Jesus lived and what he taught.[25] His teachings, as recounted in the Gospels, cover a variety of topics. Some concern human conduct: how we ought to live our lives and how we ought to treat our fellow human beings. He tells us, for example, that we ought to live according to the Golden Rule: "Always treat others as you would like them to treat you" (Matt. 7.12).[26] Such questions are

---

[25] For an excellent account of current scholarship concerning Jesus' life, see John P. Meier, *A Marginal Jew: Rethinking the Historical Jesus* (New York: Doubleday, 1991).
[26] All quotations from the Gospels are taken from the translation in *The New English Bible* (Oxford and Cambridge University Presses, 1970) unless otherwise noted. We have sometimes

matters of morality or ethics, and Jesus' views on these questions are often called his "moral" or "ethical" teachings. Other teachings concern God, God's relation to us and to our world, and God's relation to Jesus himself. Jesus claims, for example, to be the Son of God and says that God has sent him into our world to save us from our sins. Since theology is the study of God, these later teachings might be called Jesus' "theological" teachings.

One might adopt various attitudes toward Jesus' teachings. One might regard his moral and his theological teachings as two parts of the same package and either accept or reject both together. However, a fairly common response today is to accept his moral teachings, but to reject his theological ones. People who adopt this selective response might be seen as being willing to meet Jesus halfway. They honor him as a great teacher of morality, even while remaining skeptical about him as a teacher of theology.

C. S. Lewis (1893–1963), a professor of medieval and renaissance literature of Cambridge University, author of numerous scholarly and popular books, and one of the most articulate defenders of traditional Christianity in the twentieth century, has hard words for people who take up this view of Jesus. In a collection of lectures titled "What Christians Believe," he writes:

> I am trying here to prevent anyone saying the really foolish thing that people often say about Him: "I'm ready to accept Jesus as a great teacher, but I don't accept his claim to be God." That is the one thing we must not say. A man who was merely a man and said the sort of things Jesus said would not be a great moral teacher. He would be a lunatic. . . . You must make your choice. Either this man was, and is the Son of God: or else a madman or something worse. You can shut Him up for a fool . . . or you can fall at His feet and call him Lord and God. But let us not come with any patronizing nonsense about his being a great human teacher. He has not left that open to us. He did not intend to.[27]

---

have use of the King James Version in the case of passages that are especially familiar in that translation.

[27] C. S. Lewis, *Mere Christianity* (New York: MacMillan, 1952).

What is Lewis saying here? Though this isn't all he wants to say, part of his point seems to be that what we have called Jesus' moral and his theological teaching have to be accepted or rejected as a package—that the moral teachings make no sense apart from the theological teachings. That, at any rate, is the point that we shall take as the focus of our discussion in this chapter. We shall ask, first, exactly what Jesus does teach in the Gospels about how we should live our lives in this world and how we should deal with the problems that confront us in this world. We shall then ask whether, on the basis of these teachings, it is reasonable to regard Jesus as a great moral teacher? We shall argue that this is not reasonable. We shall try to show that, as Lewis suggests, the moral teachings do not make much sense when they are taken out of the context of the rest of his message. Like Lewis, we shall maintain that one should not accept Jesus as a great moral teacher unless one also accepts his theological teachings.

THE MORAL TEACHINGS OF JESUS

What sort of vision of human life in this world and of relations among human beings does Jesus present in the Gospels? Surely his dominant theme is the importance of love. When asked which is the greatest of God's commandments, he replies:

> "Love the Lord your God with all you heart, with all your soul, with all your mind." That is the greatest commandment. It comes first. There is a second like it: "Love your neighbor as yourself." Everything in the Law and the Prophets hangs on these two commandments. (Matt. 22.37–40)

Love of one's neighbor ranks only behind love of God in importance, and Jesus proclaims it as the guiding principle of all human relationships.

Jesus makes two things clear about this second greatest commandment in his teachings and by his example. First, your neighbors are not merely those who live near you, who are like you, or who share your beliefs and values. All human beings are your neighbors. In fact, he says that the neighbors whom you ought to love as you do yourself include those who do not love you:

> If you love only those who love you, what credit is that to you? Even sinners love those who love them. Again, if you do good only to those who do good to you, what credit is that to you? Even sinners do as much . . . But you must love your enemies . . . and you will have a rich reward: you will be children of the Most High, because he himself is kind to the ungrateful and the wicked. (Luke 6.32–36)

Second, loving your neighbors means helping them. The love he has in mind finds its expression, not just in friendly feelings, but in feeding the hungry, clothing the naked, and comforting the sick (Jesus puts both points vividly in his famous parable of the Good Samaritan in Luke 10.29–37). In his view, obedience to God's commandment requires a life of practical service to all those who need our help.

Jesus' insistence on the overwhelming importance of love in all human relationships is undoubtedly what people have in mind when they call him a great moral teacher. But, however admirable this teaching, we require further guidance if we are to put it into effect in our day-to-day lives. If I am to devote myself to helping others, how can I best manage my time, resources, and individual abilities so as to do them the most good? What sort of help would do them the most good? What should I do when confronted with people who do not love their neighbors as themselves, with people who oppress or exploit their neighbors? When we turn to these questions, Jesus' status as a great moral teacher begins to seem more questionable.

RESIST NOT EVIL

Let us take up the questions raised above in reverse order. A problem to which every system of morality needs an answer is the question of what to do about injustice. Injustice can appear in many forms. Often it takes the form of wrongs done by one person to another for purely personal motives. Ordinary criminal offenses such as robbery, rape, and murder fit into this category. But injustice can also appear in more systematic forms. There can be unjust social institutions or practices, such as slavery; unjust forms of government, such as dictatorship; and unjust laws, such as laws which deprive people of freedom of speech, or which enforce racial discrimination. What does Jesus teach about how we ought to respond when confronted by individual or institutional injustice?

The world into which Jesus was born contained numerous and quite dramatic instances of institutional injustice. He lived out his life on earth in a land oppressed by foreign military rule. About half a century before his birth, the Romans had come to the Holy Land as conquerors, and they continued to rule it during his life, either directly through a military governor (the procurator) in Jerusalem, or indirectly through local collaborators dependent on Roman power, as in Jesus' home territory of Galilee. Indeed, Jesus met his death on the orders of the Roman procurator Pontius Pilate. Roman rule involved crushing taxation, forced labor, and frequent massacres of those who refused to comply with such measures. It was bitterly resented by most of the Jewish population and violently resisted by some of them.[28]

As described in the last chapter, a few decades after Jesus' trial before Pilate, Jewish resentment against Roman rule boiled over into a general revolt. The Roman generals Vespasian and Titus crushed this revolt with great slaughter and destroyed the temple in Jerusalem that is so often mentioned in the Gospels. Even this victory failed to quell the spirit of Jewish resistance and, following a second major revolt in 132 CE, the Romans drove much of the Jewish population into permanent exile from the Holy Land.

Despite the manifest injustice of Roman rule, the Gospels do not record that Jesus ever denounced it or encouraged any form of resistance against it. To the contrary, when he comments on the practice

---

[28] Descriptions of political and social conditions in the eastern Mediterranean lands during Jesus' day are found in J. D. Crosson, *The Historical Jesus* (San Francisco: Harper, 1991) and in R. A. Horsley and J. S. Hanson, *Bandits, Prophets, and Messiahs: Popular Movements of the Time of Jesus* (San Francisco: Harper, 1985).

of forcing the local inhabitants to carry the Roman army's baggage when it moved from town to town, he says, "If a man in authority makes you go one mile, go with him two" (Matt 5.41). This is the origin of the expression, "Going the extra mile." When the Pharisees ask him whether it is right to pay taxes to Caesar (i.e., to the Roman emperor), Jesus replies:

> "Show me the money in which the tax is paid." They handed him a silver piece. Jesus asked, "whose head is this and whose inscription?" "Caesar's," they replied. He said to them, "Then pay Caesar what is due to Caesar, and pay God what is due to God." (Matt. 22.19–21)

Even when confronted with one of the atrocities of Roman rule— Pilate's massacre of Galileans on a pilgrimage to the temple—Jesus counsels his hearers to look to their own evil rather than Pilate's.

> At that time there were some people present who told him about the Galileans whose blood Pilate had mixed with their sacrifices. He answered them: "Do you think that, because these Galileans suffered this fate, they must have been greater sinners than anyone else in Galilee? I tell you they were not; but unless you repent, you will all come to the same end." (Luke 13.1–5)

A second form of institutional injustice on which Jesus might have commented was slavery. Slavery was perhaps the most pervasive social evil of the ancient Mediterranean world. Romans, Greeks, and Jews who could afford to do so generally owned slaves. Slaves did much of the labor necessary to support ancient civilization, and a large percentage of the population throughout the Roman world lived and died in slavery. Though slavery enjoyed the support of law and custom, many enlightened thinkers of the day denounced it, and Rome was often troubled by slave revolts, such as the one led by Spartacus in the first century BCE.

Jesus was, of course, well aware of slavery. Several of his parables mention relations between masters and slaves, for example, the story of the master who leaves money for his servants to invest for him

(Matt. 25). Interestingly, in this parable he uses the relation of master to slave as an analogy for the relation of God to human beings. Yet nowhere in the Gospels does Jesus explicitly denounce the institution of slavery. He seems to take its existence for granted. Paul, one of the greatest figures of the early Christian movement, saw no inconsistency between the teachings of Jesus and Paul's own injunction:

> Slaves, give entire obedience to your earthly masters, not merely as an outward show of service, to carry favor with men, but with single-mindedness, out of reverence for the Lord. Whatever you are doing, put your whole heart into it, as if you were doing it for the Lord and not for men knowing that there is a master who will give you . . . a reward for your services. Christ is the master whose slaves you must be. (Col. 3.22–24)

One might respond to the above observations by arguing that because Jesus had already condemned Roman oppression or ancient slavery implicitly, he did not need to do so explicitly. When he tells us to love our neighbors as ourselves and to treat others as we would like others to treat us, he endorses general principles that are incompatible with military dictatorship and slavery. No one who lives according to the Golden Rule would oppress others or deliberately exploit and humiliate them. If we all took Jesus' teachings as our guide, evils such as tyranny and slavery could never arise.

This reply has some force, but it overlooks two problems. First, one might wonder whether it is enough to condemn clear and present evils merely by implication. Suppose that a citizen of Nazi Germany, for example, endorsed the Golden Rule but neglected to specifically condemn the Nazi genocide against the Jews. Though even to do this much might take some courage, one might question whether it represents an adequate response to such an obvious and terrible evil. Second, though it's true that universal compliance with the Golden Rule would make the institution of slavery impossible, it is also true (as Jesus understood quite well) that such universal compliance is extremely unlikely. What should we do when we encounter institutions which operate in defiance of the Golden Rule? Should we publicly denounce them? Should we act, individually or collectively, to overthrow them? To simply urge that everyone live by the Golden Rule is to leave these questions unanswered.

Again, one might argue that, in endorsing the Golden Rule, Jesus implicitly calls on us to resist and struggle to eliminate injustice. But Jesus himself seems to draw no such conclusion from his teachings. In one of his most memorable and powerful passages (here, from the King James translation of his Sermon on the Mount), he contrasts his own teachings with the accepted morality of his day:

> Ye have heard that it hath been said, thou shalt love thy neighbor and hate thine enemy. But I say unto you, love your enemies, bless them that curse you, do good to them that hate you, and pray for them that despitefully use you and persecute you; that you may be children of your Father which is in heaven; for he maketh his sun to rise on the evil and on the good and sendth rain on the just and on the unjust. (Matt. 5.38–40, 43–45)

Jesus' teaching about how we should deal with evil is straightforward, though we might find it hard to accept. Look to the evil in yourselves, he tells us. Repent and reform your own conduct. Do not judge other people, leave judgment to God. (Matt. 7.1) When others treat you unjustly, do not resist. Accept and forgive. Although one might stand in awe of the self-discipline and even the heroism required in order to live according to this teaching, one might also question whether it represents the best way of dealing with injustice. Would it not be better sometimes to resist injustice, and to act to protect oneself and others against it? Many Christians have thought so. Christians (and even some non-Christians) involved in the nineteenth century struggle to abolish slavery, the twentieth century campaign for civil rights in the United States and South Africa, and the contemporary resistance to tyranny in Eastern Europe, China, and Latin America have often invoked to teachings of Jesus in support of their actions. But it is not clear how much support can be found in the Gospels for active, effective resistance to injustice.

THE POOR YOU HAVE WITH YOU ALWAYS

The Gospels speak again and again of Jesus' personal compassion for the poor and of the great value he attaches to works of charity. Yet they offer little guidance on the question of how to deal with the general problem of poverty. Nearly all human societies face the problem of what to do to help the poor. This problem confronts even wealthy modern nations, such as the United States, and it was all the more pressing in Jesus' own day. The vast majority of people in Jesus' world lived under constant threat of starvation and destitution. However, beyond recommending personal giving and direct aid, Jesus says nothing about what we might do collectively to eliminate the factors responsible for this condition. (For a contrasting account, see Mohammed's approach to this problem in chapter 4.)

Of course, one might argue that if all those who are well-off were to share their personal resources with those in need, the problem of poverty would be solved automatically. Perhaps in societies such as ours where most people have more than enough resources to satisfy their own basic needs, a personal commitment to charity would be all that is required. But in Jesus' day, the total resources available to society would not have been adequate to secure the satisfaction of everyone's basic needs, no matter how equally those resources were distributed. Even in our own time, if we look to the worldwide problem of poverty, few people believe that the problem could be solved simply by encouraging a charitable redistribution of existing resources. It is for that reason that contemporary efforts to alleviate poverty focus on promoting education, on population control, as well as on solicitation of charitable contributions from wealthy individuals.

These sorts of concerns are notably absent from Jesus' teachings about poverty. He miraculously feeds five thousand people with a few loaves and fishes, but offers no advice about how to organize agricultural production so that everyone will have enough to eat. He heals many sick people, but says nothing about what we should do to insure that everyone receives adequate health care.

Nor does it seem that Jesus intends his call to each of us to feed the hungry and cloth the naked as part of some general program for eliminating poverty. The Gospels recount the story of a woman who anointed Jesus with a very expensive perfumed oil. Some of those who witnessed her action rebuked her. They told her that her action was wasteful and pointed out that she might have sold the perfume and donated the money to the poor.

> But Jesus said, "Let her alone.... It is a fine thing that she has done for me. You have the poor among you always and you can help them whenever you like; but you will not always have me." (Mark 14.6–7)

Had Jesus seen his teaching on charity primarily as part of a plan for eliminating poverty, one might have expected him to at least acknowledge the justice of the principle to which the woman's critics appeal.

Likewise, Jesus' warnings against accumulation of riches seem to be motivated more by concern for the souls of the wealthy than by the hope of ending poverty through redistribution of income. When a rich young man declines the invitation to give all his property to the poor and follow Jesus, Jesus does not express regret that the poor have been deprived of the rich man's contribution. Rather, he remarks on how difficult it is for the rich to enter the Kingdom of Heaven (Matt 19.16–26). His view is that the pursuit of riches distracts one from more important concerns. "For even when a man has more than enough, his wealth does not give him life" (Luke 12.15). Don't set your heart on riches, instead,

> Sell your possessions and give in charity. Provide for yourselves ... never-failing wealth in heaven, where no thief can steal it and no moth destroy it. For where your wealth is, there will your heart be also. (Luke 12.3–34)

Jesus ultimately recommends charitable giving more for its effects on the giver than for the benefits it confers on the receiver.

CONSIDER THE LILIES OF THE FIELD

Suppose that the rich young man had given away all his possessions in obedience to Jesus' admonition. How would he then have survived? What would have happened to his family? An old maxim, found nowhere in the Bible, says that the Lord helps those who help themselves. Do we not need to take some responsibility for our own well-being and for that of those dependent on us? Is it right for us to live on the charity of others, if we have the ability to support ourselves? Might not the rich young man have made a greater contribution to his community by, say, founding a business that employed many people than by giving away all he owned? Though morality often requires us to sacrifice our interests for the sake of others, it must also acknowledge our legitimate concerns for our own welfare. Those who have no concern for themselves are likely to become a drain on public resources.

Jesus seems to have little use for this sort of prudent, responsible approach to life. Another of the best known passages from the King James Version of the Bible eloquently sums up his teachings on this topic:

> Therefore I say unto you, take no thought for your life, what ye shall eat, or what ye shall drink; nor yet for your body, what ye shall put on. . . . Behold the fowls of the air: for they sow not, neither do they reap, nor gather into barns; yet your heavenly Father feedeth them. Are ye not much better than they? Which of you by taking thought can add one cubit unto his stature? And why take ye thought for raiment? Consider the lilies of the field, how they grow; they toil not, neither do they spin. And yet I say unto you, that even Solomon in all his glory was not arrayed like one of these. Wherefore, if God so clothe the grass of the field . . . shall he not much more clothe you, O ye of little faith? Therefore, take no thought, saying, what shall we eat? Or what shall we drink? Or wherewithal shall we be clothed? . . . But seek ye first the kingdom of God, and his righteousness: and all these things shall be added unto you; Take, therefore, no thought for the morrow: for the morrow shall take thought for the things of itself. (Matt. 6.25–34)

A Preliminary Evaluation of Jesus' Moral Teachings

As presented in the preceding section of the chapter, Jesus' moral teachings seem to include some highly questionable doctrines. He tells us not to resist evil, and apparently recommends passive acceptance and forgiveness as our primary response to social injustice. He endorses charity toward the poor, but gives us little practical guidance about what we can do to eliminate poverty. He advises us to take no thought concerning our material welfare and simply to trust that God will provide for us. However much one might admire his teachings on love, forgiveness, and humility, his moral vision seems alarmingly limited and incomplete. It seems clear that, in order to make our world a better place, we must struggle diligently against injustice. We must think systematically and intelligently about how to ameliorate evils such as poverty and disease. We must take responsibility for our own welfare insofar as we are able. Jesus seems not to recognize these needs, or to be indifferent to them. Surely a great moral teacher ought to speak to them more effectively than Jesus does in the Gospels.

Have we, perhaps, distorted Jesus' moral teachings? Not, we hope, the teachings themselves. We have done our best to present fairly the particular teachings discussed above. As far as possible, we have relied on Jesus' own words as recorded in the Gospels. But in another way, our presentation represents a deliberate distortion. We have taken his teaching out of the context in which they occur in the Gospels. In the Gospels his teachings about how human beings ought to live their lives in this world form one part of a much larger picture or worldview. That picture also includes Jesus' teachings about God and about God's plan for us and about Jesus' own role in those plans.

We have deliberately lifted his moral teachings out of the more general picture presented in the Gospels so that we can focus attention on the question that began this chapter, that is, do those doctrines in themselves, independent of Jesus' other views, justify the conclusion that Jesus was a great moral teacher? Or, put in other words, could one reasonably accept Jesus as a great moral teacher, while rejecting his claims to be the Son of God?

Lewis asserts that the answer is no. It seems to us that there is a good deal to be said for Lewis's position. If we look at Jesus' moral teachings in isolation, they represent a seriously inadequate account of how we ought to deal with the problems of a world marred by injustice and limitations of resources. Turning the other cheek, giving all your possessions to the poor, and taking no thought for tomorrow hardly constitute an effective plan for creating a better world. However, it may be that this plan would seem far more reasonable if it were examined in the context of Jesus' other teachings. It is to that context which we now turn our attention.

THE COMING OF THE KINGDOM

We have remarked that the Gospels fail to adequately instruct us about what we must do to make the world a better place. Perhaps the reason is that making the world a better place is not supposed to be our job. Whose job is it then? According to Jesus, it is God's job and he will do more than reform the world. He will bring the world as we know it to an end.

Jesus began his ministry by proclaiming, "Repent, for the Kingdom of Heaven is at hand" (Matt. 4.17). In the Gospels of Matthew, Mark, and Luke, he repeats this message again and again. It is the good news (i.e., the Gospel) that he charges his disciples to preach to all people. What is this kingdom whose coming he announces? New Testament scholars differ regarding the full meaning of the phrase, but Jesus makes clear that the coming of the Kingdom of Heaven involves a radical transformation of human existence.

Shortly before his arrest and crucifixion, he tells his disciples what to expect when he has gone. He warns of a time of troubles to come, a time of war, famine, and natural disasters. Those calamities represent, he says, "the birth pangs of the new age" (Matt. 24.9). Those who follow him will be persecuted for their faith, but at last, "this gospel of the kingdom will be proclaimed throughout the earth and then the end will come" (Matt. 24.14). The sun will darken, the moon will not give her light, and the stars will fall from the sky: "All the peoples of the world will see the Son of Man coming on the clouds of heaven with great power and glory" (Matt. 24.30).

Jesus does not claim to know exactly when he will return, but he expects it to be soon. "I tell you this," he warns the disciples, "the present generation will live to see it all. . . . But about that day and hour no one knows, not even the angels in heaven, not even the Son; only the Father" (Matt. 24.34–36). Therefore, he urges them to be watchful: "Keep awake, then; for you do not know on what day your Lord is to come" (Matt. 24.42).

When he returns he will sit in judgment over all humanity. To those who have believed in him and in his teachings he will say, "you have my Father's blessing; come, enter and possess the kingdom that has been ready for you since the world was made" (Matt. 25.34). On those who have rejected him and his teaching, he will pronounce a curse: "The curse is upon you: go from my sight into the eternal fire that is ready for the Devil and his angels" (Matt. 25.41). And the accursed ones "will go away to eternal punishment, but the righteous into eternal life" (Matt. 25.46). Inside the kingdom will be perfect peace and contentment under God's protection; outside it, darkness, wailing, gnashing of teeth, and spiritual death.

For the righteous, the coming of the kingdom represents the solution to all their problems, but it is a solution not of their own making. The coming of the kingdom is God's doing, not our doing. It will come when God wills it. Human action can neither bring it about, nor hold it back. What our actions determine is whether we shall have a place in the kingdom or remain outside it. We face a momentous choice: eternal life in the kingdom or eternal punishment in Hell. Whatever distracts us from this choice is a millstone around our necks. We must cut off and cast away everything that holds us back from making a wholehearted, singleminded commitment to do what it takes to enter into the kingdom.

> If thy hand offend thee, cut it off: it is better for thee to enter into life maimed, than having two hands to go into hell. . . . And if thy foot offend

thee, cut it off; it is better for thee to enter half into life than having two feet to be cast into hell. . . . And if thy eye offend thee, pluck it out; it is better for thee to enter the Kingdom of God with one eye than having two eyes to be cast into hell fire. (Mark 9.43–47, King James Version)

Since the coming judgment will decide our fate for all time, we must let nothing stand in our way.

If we put Jesus' moral teachings in the context of his prophesy of the coming of the kingdom, doctrines that seem unreasonable in isolation begin to make perfect sense. Why should we bother to resist injustice? The evil that we have to fear is not the evil that's done to us by others, but the evil in ourselves. Being oppressed or exploited by others will not cost us our place in God's kingdom, but our own sins will condemn us to the outer darkness. Hence Jesus' advice to look to the evil in ourselves rather than worry about the evil done by others. Eliminating injustice from the world is not our job. God will settle all accounts at the last judgment.

Likewise, poverty and other forms of human misery will disappear (for the righteous) with the coming of the kingdom. This is why Jesus does not try to teach us what we must do in order to eliminate poverty. Jesus does not recommend individual acts of charity as part of a program for raising the average standard of living through redistribution of income. The point is rather for the giver to demonstrate love of God's creatures and obedience to God's commands; thus the giver lays up treasures in Heaven.

This context also explains why Jesus recommends an apparently imprudent and irresponsible attitude toward concerns for our material well-being. The person who takes no thought for tomorrow, who does not ask, "What shall I eat? What shall I drink? What shall I wear?," but instead trusts that God will provide, is not being imprudent. Rather, this person is attending to the things that really matter. Whether you enter into the kingdom does not depend on your bodily health, or your material prosperity, but on your trust in God. The rich young man does not exercise prudence when he holds on to his possessions rather than follow Jesus. Rather, he irresponsibly throws away his chance at eternal salvation.

If we suppose that Jesus' teachings in the Gospels provide a pre-scription for making the world a better place by means of human action, then that prescription will seem a very inadequate remedy for the problems that we face in this world. But he is not telling us what we have to do to make this world a better place. He is telling us what we must do to be saved when this world comes to an end. If we accept Jesus' teaching as a whole, then it is the latter problem with which we are faced. God will reform the world; we need only worry about reforming ourselves.

On the other hand, if we do not have good reason to trust Jesus' assurances that God will put right the evils of this world and will provide for all our needs, then following his moral teachings seems a reckless course at best. If this world is the only world we shall ever know, we ought to devote ourselves to its reform. Passive acceptance of social injustice will do irreparable harm to ourselves and to others, unless God does put things right in the end. Taking no thought for tomorrow is a prescription for disaster unless God will take care of us. So our confidence in Jesus' moral teachings must rest on our confidence that he speaks with the authority of God. This explains Lewis's insistence that, unless we regard Jesus as the Son of God, it is foolish for us to take him as our moral teacher.

CONCLUSION

We are now in a position to appreciate the point of Lewis's criticism of the view that Jesus was a great moral teacher, but not the Son of God. Jesus' teachings concerning how we ought to live our lives in this world are shaped by his acceptance of a larger picture. In that picture the world represents only a temporary residence for human beings. We shall each spend only a comparatively small portion of our existence in this world. We shall spend eternity in Heaven or Hell. Further, this temporary residence is not of our own making, and we do not control its ultimate fate. The importance of our lives in the world lies in this—that what we do here will determine whether we spend the rest of our everlasting lives in God's kingdom or outside it.

Beyond making this all-important decision, nothing else that we do here matters much. If we reform the world, but lose our immortal souls, our achievement profits us nothing; if we save our souls we gain everything, even if we fail to reform the world. For Lewis, Jesus' greatness as a teacher consists in getting us to see our lives in the context of this larger picture.

When we think about morality, we typically see our lives from a very different perspective. Here the central problem is to secure a decent, satisfying life in this world for ourselves and for our fellow human beings. We suppose that we must solve this problem by our own devices, that is, by our own intelligence, by our own will, and by our own actions. When we examine our world in this light, evils such as injustice and poverty assume an overwhelming importance. Our success as moral agents depends, if not on whether we actually solve these problems, then at least on whether we struggle diligently to find solutions for them.

If we suppose that Jesus' teachings offer us a solution to such problems, we miss the crucial point of his message. The problems of injustice and poverty might eventually be solved, but their solution does not depend on our actions. Our real problem is quite different. We should be asking ourselves, not what can we do to overcome injustice and eliminate poverty, but what must we do to be saved? This is what Jesus wants to teach us. He wants us to understand that we must deal with a problem far greater and of a very different type than the problems of morality.

So, was Jesus a great moral teacher? Lewis would say that we cannot answer this question without first deciding whether he was a great religious teacher, whether he was a great religious prophet, and whether he was the Son of God.

3

Was Jesus Divine?

▼ ▼ ▼

Paul on the Status of Jesus

The average person who knows anything about Christianity believes that Christianity makes a different claim about its founder than Judaism or Islam. That claim is that Jesus of Nazareth, the founder of the Jewish group called the Nazarenes, was more than just a prophet of God. The claim is that he was divine—the Son of God—while at the same time, one of us. In the traditional formula, the claim is that he was truly God and truly man. In this chapter, we discuss what those claims might mean and a dilemma they seem to create about atonement.

JUDAISM ON JESUS

Neither Judaism nor Islam has ever recognized the divinity of Jesus. This is not surprising because the crucial philosophical claim by Christianity is that Jesus was God. Because Christianity makes this claim, its central belief is worlds apart from Judaism and Islam.

That only a few Jews of his day recognized the divinity of Jesus embarrassed the early disciples, who were Jews and yet took great pains to blame traditional Jewish leaders for the problems of early

Christianity.[29] For example, the authors of the Gospels paint not Pilate but the Jews as responsible for the crucifixion of Jesus. Paul complains in his first letter, the earliest Christian document, about "the Jews: who both killed the Lord Jesus, and their own prophets, and have persecuted us; and they please not God, and are contrary to all men." (1 Thess. 2.14–15).

Although it is false to blame the Jews for the crucifixion of Jesus, such ideas have consequences, and this falsehood was partially responsible for later Christian persecution of Jews as "Christ-killers." Roman procurators such as Pilate were hardened rulers trained to deal with dissent harshly. They tolerated diversity of religion so long as Rome's symbolic gods were hailed, taxes were paid, and life was peaceful. Failure to meet these conditions met violent reaction. Pilate himself had already crucified hundreds of dissenters and revolutionaries. When the Roman administrator Florus heard that he had been verbally abused by Jews (after he had stolen from their temple), he crucified and killed 3,600 Jews in one day.[30]

Subsequent Christians did not always understand the orientation of the Gospel authors, who were not writing anything like reporters or historians but as evangelical writers seeking converts. They wrote twenty to seventy years after the death of Jesus during a time of great tension between those Jews who followed Jesus and those who did not. These passionate authors portray the Jews unfavorably, especially the Pharisees. Yet even in portraying the Jews in a bad light, they reveal a great deal of information. For example, John tells his Gospel readers that the natives of Galilee never accepted Jesus' words even as those of a prophet. John keeps telling us that everywhere, the Jews were very hostile to Jesus: "After these things Jesus walked in Galilee, for he would not walk in Jewry, because the Jews sought to kill him" (John 7.1).

Nor did Jesus do well in Jerusalem. When he first walked in

---

[29] "What then? Israel hath not obtained that which he seeked for; but the election hath obtained it, and the rest were blinded"; "(According as it is written, God had given them the spirit of slumber, eyes that they should not see, and ears that they should not hear;) unto this day" (The Epistle of Paul the Apostle to the Romans 11.7–8).

[30] Josephus, *The Jewish War*, trans. G. A. Williamson, ed. E. Mary Smallwood (New York: Dorset Press, 1970).

Solomon's porch portion of the temple in Jerusalem, he implied that he and YHWH were identical. Indeed, Jewish leaders explicitly accused Jesus of claiming that he was God. For that blasphemy, which John implies he had committed before in the same way, "the Jews took up stones again to stone him" (John 10.31).

Did Jesus understand himself to be God? Because we cannot enter his mind, we shall never know. Certainly he left that interpretation open among his followers ("Who do they say that I am?" he asks Peter) and even encourages it. Regardless of what Jesus himself believed (which can never be settled), later Christianity is quite clear on the matter: Jesus was part of God. Because of the importance of this view to Christianity (indeed, it becomes the central, philosophical claim of this religion), we are only concerned here with what subsequent Christianity came to understand by the relation of Jesus to God.

The crucial claim by Jesus to godhood was rejected by those who knew him best: his family, his neighbors, his countrymen of Galilee, and those who called him "rabbi," his fellow Jews. How could his followers explain this awkward fact? The answer is that they portrayed the Jews who knew Jesus as narrow-minded, obsessed by power, and obdurate ("that hearing they may hear, and not understand").[31]

THE STATUS OF JESUS

Because his epistles or letters are the earliest documents of Christianity, we probably know more about Paul than we know about Jesus. Born about the same time as Jesus into a Jewish family, Saul grew up in the city of Tarsus, which was several days' journey north of Jerusalem and the center of Hellenism in the Middle East.[32] He was raised

---

[31] See above reference to Romans 11.7–8. See also Romans 10.1–4, 11.25. Sometimes wavering Christians today wish that God would appear to them personally, so that they might have secure faith. The awkward fact for Christians is that, according to the Gospels, Jesus did exactly that. Even with this *theophany*, his neighbors, family, and disciples did not recognize him as God.
[32] Michael Grant, *Saint Paul* (New York: Crossroad Publishing, 1982), p. 13.

in a middle-class, educated family, where his father was a textile merchant. His father must have been an important man, for the family had been granted Roman citizenship.

In Tarsus, Saul learned to write. As such he was an extremely rare, valuable person in the ancient world. More important, he read and wrote in Greek, the dominant language of Hellenic culture and world trade (his epistles are in Greek, as are the original versions of the Gospels).[33]

To say this is not to say that Paul grew up in a Hellenistic family. He was raised as a Jew and became a Pharisee. As he writes in his epistles, he was a stickler for the law in his early years.

Some time after the crucifixion of Jesus (circa 30 CE), Saul vigorously persecuted the small group of Jewish Nazarenes who had become disciples of Jesus of Nazareth. Although the author of Acts reports that Saul helped in the stoning of the disciple Stephen, that story is almost certainly an exaggeration in the literal sense. Nevertheless, Saul certainly helped to organize and reward those who persecuted the early followers of Jesus.

Shortly after the death of Stephen, Saul embarked on a journey to Damascus. On this trip, Paul later writes in Galatians, Jesus revealed himself to Paul: "But I certify you, brethren, that the gospel which was preached of me is not after man. For I neither received it of man, neither was I taught it, but by the revelation of Jesus Christ" (1.11–12). Some of those with Paul claim to have seen nothing but to have heard something; others claim to have seen something but heard nothing. The Greek word for "seeing" used in Paul's letters is ambiguous and allows both internal and normal external seeing.

This manifestation was so overwhelming that Saul on the spot converted to the Nazarenes, henceforth abandoning his Jewish name and adopting its Greek version, Paul. Paul then traveled on to Damascus and attempted to join the Christian community, but was prevented from doing so by being evicted from the city by either the orthodox Jews or the procurator of the Romans. For the next ten to

---

[33] It is possible that Matthew existed in Hebrew, but we now only have Greek versions. It is also possible that the Hebrew was translated from the Greek.

fifteen years, he traveled around Arabia and we know little about what he did or why.

About 45 CE, he took his first journey through Syria and lower Asia Minor, attempting to convert Jews to the new sect. He met with miserable failure among the Jews, but found the Greek-speaking peoples of this area very receptive. A second journey took him to Greece and Macedonia and lasted three years.

While he was gone, the Nazarenes developed schisms, the chief of which concerned whether non-Jews such as Samaritans and Greeks could be saved.[34] If not, then the Nazarenes did not want to eat with them, let their daughters marry among them, or have them in their synagogues. In the first council of this fledgling sect, the Council of Jerusalem, Paul asserted a view that has today become known as his "Gentile Mission."

The writers of the Gospels report Jesus as saying different things about whether non-Jews (or Gentiles) could be saved and enter the Kingdom of God. Matthew writes that Jesus said, "Go nowhere among the Gentiles, and enter no town of the Samaritans, but go rather to the lost sheep of the House of Israel" (10.5–6). Other passages seem to imply that some non-Jews could also be saved (Matt. 8.11; John 4.23–26, 39–42).

In any case, early converts to Jesus first had to convert to Judaism. For the roughly twenty years between the death of Jesus in approximately 30–33 CE and the Council of Jerusalem in 50 CE, male Gentiles accepting the message of Jesus had to become circumcised, follow the Mosaic laws, and marry only Jews—standard criteria of being Jewish.

Regardless of whether this was implicit in the message of Jesus, it was Paul's genius to explicitly waive this entry requirement. Paul presents himself in his letter to the Romans as "the minister of Jesus to the Gentiles" (15.16). Christianity would never have become the official religion of Rome and Europe if Paul had not had this Gentile Mission and if Greeks had first been required to convert to Judaism.

---

[34] See Acts 15.1–5. See also Paul Johnson, *A History of Christianity* (New York: Atheneum, 1983), chap. 1.

Without Paul's change, the Roman emperor Constantine would never have converted to Christianity around 300 CE, and without his conversion, Europe might not have gone Christian.

Paul also began the anti-Semitic view in Christianity. Like an ex-smoker who reserves his greatest rancor for those still smoking, Paul smarted when his former Jewish friends and colleagues would not accept his revelation on the road to Damascus. It was as if they were calling him a liar, and this rejection provoked a special wrath in him. The earliest work in the New Testament (written about 51 CE) is Paul's letter to the Thessalonians, where he writes that the Jews are those, "Who killed the Lord Jesus, and their own prophets, and have persecuted us; and they please not God, and are contrary to all men" (2.15).

It is not surprising, then, that when Paul returned to Jerusalem in 58 CE, the Jews there tried to kill him. The Roman administration prevented his death, but Jewish leaders succeeded in having him imprisoned for two years in a nearby city.

As a Roman citizen, Paul requested an appeal of his sentence at the emperor's court in Rome, which was granted. On his way there by ship, he was shipwrecked and washed up on the shores of the island of Malta, where he spent a cold winter. When he got to Rome, it is unclear exactly what happened, but he appears to have been imprisoned for several years. He probably died in Rome, perhaps as a part of making the early Christians a scapegoat for Nero's great fire in 64 CE.[35]

In personality, Paul was a tortured soul, a conflicted man torn between a confidence in his own talents that bordered on arrogance and his self-imposed, fledgling, Christian humility. He was undoubtedly a man of great mental powers and was the first to understand that the new Nazarenes could be not just a new sect of Judaism, or even a reformation of Judaism, but a new religion. Moreover, he certainly understood that such a new religion had the possibility to escape the ethnic confines of the Jewish YHWH and his territorial limitations. Given what Greek culture had accomplished in the previous three

---

[35] Ibid., p. 21.

centuries of Hellenization, and how his home city of Tarsus was a Hellenistic center, Paul must have realized how easily this new cult of Jesus could graft onto the universalism of Greek culture.

Paul also emphasized the sinfulness of human nature: "For sin . . . deceived me, and by it slew me" (Romans 7.11). This means that humans typically will not reach Heaven without help from Jesus. People are led astray by sex, jealousy, money, and concerns of the world; they forget too easily about the primacy of their relation to God. For Paul, the relation between a person and God was a deep, almost unbridgeable chasm. Here is a concept of God that is seen later in Islam, which stresses God's glory and magnificence, but at a price of making God distant and impersonal.

Jesus here is the supreme intermediary as a being both divine and human who bridges the gulf between this and the divine world. In Jesus, God "reconciles the world to himself," and in turn, Jesus is the "door" for humans to reach God: "For if we believe that Jesus died and rose again, even so them also which sleep in Jesus will God bring with him." (1 Thess. 4.14) So later John emphasizes that Jesus said, "I am the way, the truth, and the life; no one comes to the Father, but by me" (John 14.6). For Paul, Jesus bridges the gap, making God accessible. For Paul, Jesus makes God personal.

Conjoining the notion of sin with the mediating role of Jesus brings us to Paul's emphasis on the suffering of Jesus. Jesus is the Redeemer, Paul says, and by his suffering death, we can be saved. Paul stresses that what allows sin to be forgiven is the sacrifice of Jesus. By his suffering on the cross, human salvation is possible. For Paul, Christianity's God would be the same as Allah were it not for the redemptive role of Jesus. When asked what it means to be a Christian, Christians say, "You must accept Jesus as your savior." How is he a savior? The reply is, "He suffered and died for my sins." This is the Doctrine of Atonement, the view that Jesus atoned for our sins by voluntarily going through his agonized death.

On this Paul says explicitly,

> But God commandeth his love toward us, in that, while we were yet sinners, Christ died for us.

> Much more then, being now justified by his blood, we shall be saved
> from wrath through him.
>
> . . .
>
> And not only so, but we also joy in God through our Lord Jesus
> Christ, by whom we have now received the atonement. (Rom. 5.8,
> 9, 11)

In later Christian theology, the suffering of Jesus is absolutely crucial.
If there was not suffering by Jesus, the scales could not be balanced.
The immense quantity of human sin in the world requires an immense, superhuman compensation. For this reason, medieval art later
emphasizes the immense physical agony of Jesus on the cross.[36] For
this reason, indulgences are later sold, drawing on the infinite pool of
forgiveness earned by Jesus. For this reason—Paul says with fierce
intensity—humanity is saved.

Incarnation or Atonement?

The study of the nature of Jesus, especially in regard to God, is called
Christology. Paul emphatically asserts that Jesus was divine. Paul says
Jesus did not merely later become a God when he first appeared in the
temple or on the cross. For Paul, Jesus was God's son, born incarnate, or
in the flesh, in Mary's womb. This is the Doctrine of the Incarnation.

Consider two groups of Christians who lived at the time of Jesus
and who both rejected the Doctrine of the Incarnation. First, the
Ebionites were a group of Jewish Christians who did not believe that
Jesus had been part of God because they accepted the Doctrine of
Atonement. Because Jesus really did suffer, humanity's sins are forgiven. Because no superhuman, divine being can really suffer, Jesus
was not divine.

Another group, the Docetists, believed that Jesus really was part of
God but that no part of God was really in the flesh. The name
"Docetist" comes from the ancient Greek word for mask, *docere*, and

---

[36] *Oxford Illustrated History of Christianity* (New York: Oxford University Press, 1990), p. 221.
This suffering is especially emphasized in the late Carolingian period.

the Docetists believed that God adopted the mask of human flesh to convey his message to humanity. But no part of God was in the flesh in Mary's womb nor was he ever, say, a little child who played at children's games. For both Ebionites and Docetists, God did not, as Jesus, become a human incarnate.

Paul surely knew about both of these interpretations and mightily rejected both. Paul's uncompromising view created massive problems for the future of Christianity. Like the Ebionites, many Jews seem to have accepted the message of Jesus but would not go so far as to say that Jesus was actually God. For almost all the Jews who knew Jesus, this was just too much. Like later Moslems, many Jews at Jerusalem thought that Jesus was a great, gifted prophet of God, but not part of God, not divine, and certainly not God himself.

Yet Paul claimed that Jesus was divine and of the same holy status as God, even in being tempted by Satan and on the cross. If Jesus was indeed divine, the Docetists asked, how could he suffer? If Jesus was part of God, what was happening on the cross when Jesus cries out: "Eli, Eli, lama sabachthani?"[37] Why did he ask why his Father had forsaken him? Was this just a charade? Or was God here just wearing the mask of a human body, as the Docetists asserted? When Jesus says, "Father, forgive them; for they know not what they do" (Luke 23.42), who is he asking, himself?

Is God acting for benefit of the onlookers? If so, isn't it deceitful? Or is this a brief moment, as the Jews probably see it, when a crazy Jesus suddenly gains his sanity and asks God for help? Or do the words on the cross show, as some scholars claim, that Jesus never thought of himself as identical with God? If so, a central claim of later Christianity is false.

Those opposed to Paul, and they included most Jews of his time, reasoned like this:

1. Either Jesus was not divine, or Jesus did not suffer on the Cross.

---

[37] "My God, my God. Why hast Thou forsaken me?" (Jesus of course did not speak in English). Mark 15.34

2. If Jesus did not suffer on the Cross, then Jesus did not earn forgiveness for humanity's sins.

3. If Jesus did not earn forgiveness for sin, then Jesus cannot redeem mankind.

Later Jews and Moslems added a fourth point: Only God can help humans, not a mere prophet.

Suppose we reject the premise that Jesus did not suffer on the cross. That is, suppose we instead assert that he did suffer. In that case, Jesus is human and fallible. He is like Moses and Mohammed. This explains why Jesus incorrectly forecast the imminent coming of the Kingdom of God. When Jesus prayed, his Father was in Heaven. In Paul's view, such prayer is problematic because Jesus is of the same holy nature as Abba, "the Father."

If this (Ebionite) route of the philosophical fork is taken, a very high toll must be paid. After the death of Jesus, many of his followers began to drift back into the orthodox Jewish synagogues. Even James, the very brother of Jesus, incurs Paul's wrath by appearing to accept the interpretation that there is not much difference between the great Jewish prophets and Jesus. This line of reasoning leads toward Judaism or Islam.

Paul changes all that by insisting that Jesus was not just another great prophet. Paul stresses that Jesus was actually divine and a part or son of God.

The exact nature of this relationship is very confusing and a problem in later Christianity, especially when it is asserted that Jesus and God are not only of the same holy nature, but an identical substance. This Doctrine of the Trinity (which added the Holy Spirit as also identical) caused great dissent and controversy among people who could not accept it. But that is getting ahead of our story and is not our concern here.

We are not discussing here the identity of Jesus with God, as the doctrine of the Trinity asserts, but merely the divine nature or godhood of Jesus. If Jesus is just another prophet—just a man—then the heart of Christianity is false. Christianity as a religion separate from Judaism is founded on this philosophical belief. Paul establishes his

Christ-centered view as a new religion not only by his Gentile Mission but by putting all his strength on the one point that Judaism could never accept: the deity of the man Jesus. Later Moslems also side with Jews on just this point against Paul.[38]

OTHER PROBLEMS ABOUT THE NATURE OF JESUS

The issue of Jesus' suffering has always been a big stumbling block for anyone thinking about the status of Jesus. First, there is the problem of the mental suffering. For anyone unfortunate enough to face a situation calling for great courage, part of what makes an act courageous is taking risk in the face of the unknown. Suppose a scientist exposes a fellow scientist in his large company who has been faking safety data. Such a person is a hero in part because such people are commonly penalized for their actions (they are often fired). But suppose the whistleblower had secret knowledge that he would be promoted for his action, for example, that a new ethical president was about to take office and that he wanted to rid his company of corrupt scientists. In that case, the action of the whistleblower would not be heroic but self-promoting.

Similarly, if Jesus knows that he runs no risk of dying on the cross, is

[38] Both Jews and Moslems later wonder pointedly why they should believe Paul. If everything hangs on Paul's radically different interpretation of the words of Jesus, if there is no independent corroborating evidence, if all we really have is the testimony of one man, and if such testimony came conveniently at a time when the followers of Jesus were failing, why should we believe Paul? After all, people lie (as Nietzsche implies Paul did) (Frederick Nietzsche, *The Will to Power*, trans. Walter Kaufman and R. J. Hollingdale [New York: Random House/Viking, 1968]). Nietzsche writes that Paul was a "holy epileptic" who either "falsified" (see Kaufman's translation of *The Gay Science*) or who lacked "self-criticism," such that because an idea had power to inspire people, Paul concluded that it must have been true. As such, Nietzsche writes somewhat immodestly, Paul had not "a thousandeth part of the integrity of self-criticism with which a philologist today reads a text or proves a [a point]" (*The Will to Power*, book 2, no. 171). After all, people misremember what they feel they remember with certainty. Furthermore, Paul may have been unstable, with deep feelings of guilt for his indirect role in Stephen's death: "beyond measure I persecuted the Church of God, and wasted [ravaged] it" (Galatians 1.13).

The question of Paul's accuracy differs greatly from questions about whether Jesus existed or about whether he was God. Many people saw Jesus and heard him. For Paul, we have only the strength of his inner conviction.

Nevertheless, Paul burned with sincere certainty about his mission. To his credit, he completely changed his life and never looked back. He journeyed relentlessly seeking converts and shoring up faltering churches. He probably paid ultimately with his life.

he really suffering? For any human being, the great mental agony of facing death is uncertainty about what lies after death. If Jesus runs no risk of dying, how can his actions be courageous in "posing" on the Cross?[39]

A second problem with Jesus' suffering concerns physical suffering. Certainly the passion of Jesus is commonly depicted as physical suffering, and the Catholic faithful often display crucifixes of Jesus suffering on the cross with bloodied hands, feet, and head.

The problem here is conceptual. If the essence of Jesus is essentially immaterial, in what sense can he physically suffer? Suffering the sensation of pain essentially involves having an animate body that has pain receptors, neurons, and axons to convey pain along neural pathways, and a physical brain. Can pain exist in my body and not be my pain?

If the essence of Jesus is not immaterial but body, then he can indeed suffer. And the doctrine of atonement can be true, as Paul asserts. But then we have to explain how a divine being can suffer physical pains and the emotional problems of human beings (such as anger and sadness when his disciples continuously desire miracles to prove that he is divine).

This question resembles the mind-body problem in the philosophy of René Descartes, where Cartesians must explain how an immaterial, substantial soul can experience the effect of damage to the body known as pain. How precisely does such mind-body interaction take place? Where does it occur, since the mind is at no point in space?

---

[39] Ironically, one of the few movies ever to try to make sense of the dual nature of Jesus was banned by some Christian communities. *The Last Temptation of Christ*, by the gifted director Martin Scorsese shows a Jesus struggling with both the human desires of lust and also the human yearnings of wanting a family and marital intimacy. In this movie (based on the novel by Nicholas Kazantzakis [New York: Simon & Schuster, 1960]), the suffering of Jesus is presented in a highly original way: what makes Jesus agonize most is not, as usually interpreted, his physical pain on the cross or his uncertainty about whether God has abandoned him, but rather his desire to stay human and lead a normal life of sexual fulfillment, intimacy, and human friendship. This last, of course, is precisely what he cannot have in order to fulfill his destiny. So Jesus chooses to give all this up to fulfill his role, thereby suffering perhaps more than we can know (and perhaps saving Paul's Doctrine of Atonement). It is, of course, ironic that a movie that gives such a subtle picture of a philosophical belief so central to Christianity should be banned by some Christians.

JUDAISM, PAUL, HELLENISM, AND CHRISTIANITY

From the point of view of orthodox Jews who feared the encroaching cosmopolitan glitter of Hellenism, Jesus was not the danger, but Paul. Jesus taught as as a rabbi (as his disciples call him in Mark), and his mission is as a reformer of Judaism. He takes a place in a long line of prophets going back to Nathan and Elijah, heroically risking their lives to challenge the status quo. Unlike Paul, Jesus does not address himself to Greeks but to the Jews of Palestine. Unlike Jesus, Paul is educated in the most sophisticated Greek city of Asia Minor and writes letters in Greek.

The first three Gospels, the earliest, are roughly of the same kind. Called "synoptic," they present very similar accounts of the events of the life of Jesus. Ironically, the Gospel most Christians know best is the last, probably written by the Greek John of Patmos in about 90 CE. Like Paul, this Gospel writer has long given up on the Jews and is explicitly trying to attract Hellenistic converts. To this end, he begins his Gospel not with, "In the beginning was YHWH," but instead uses the word most associated with the Greek, *logos* (i.e., "In the beginning was the Word"). The highly literary stories of John aim at converting a sophisticated, Hellenistic, non-Jewish audience.

What emerges then is that Paul, intentionally or unintentionally, founded a Hellenistic version of what he saw as the best in Jesus' version of Judaism. Paul wanted a single God with grandeur and distance from humans, a strict ethical code for daily life, a view of history, and a universal appeal. Ethical monotheism attracted possible converts and Jesus' teaching of repentance (being "born again") gave any newcomer a way to be saved. It remained to Paul to drop the traditional admission requirement, the great stumbling block of Gentiles to conversion to any form of Judaism, circumcision.

Indeed, most of his letter to the Romans can be read in this context. This letter is famous for its discussion of whether one is saved by faith or "works." But Paul's words here are not about works but about whether one is saved by "the Law" or by confessing Jesus as one's savior. The Law here means the Mosaic Law. Do you get saved by "the works of the law," Paul asks? No, he says in Romans 9.32, it is a "stumbling-stone" to the Jews. His crucial theme thereafter is that:

> For there is no difference between the Jew and the Greek: for the same Lord over all is rich unto all that call upon him.
> For whosoever shall call upon the name of the Lord shall be saved. (Rom. 10.12, 13)

Thus from an orthodox Jewish view of the first century, Paul's version of Jesus-centered Judaism was Greek-oriented, and it is not hard to see other evidence for why they must have thought this way. For example, the important early documents of Christianity are written in Greek, and more so than in other areas, the choice of language here determined the kind of thought. No one read Hebrew but the Jews, and even then, most Jews used Aramaic. Since Alexander's conquest three centuries before, Greek had been the language of the civilization of the time. It was the language one would speak to be understood almost anywhere in the world—like English today. It was the language one would use if one wanted to not reform Judaism or save Jews, but to convert Greeks to a new, more universal, less ethnic version of Judaism.

CONCLUSION

Our primary theme in this chapter has been that the core of Christian philosophical belief about Jesus contains a logical dilemma. On the one hand, there is the crucial claim that Jesus was not just another prophet, such as Moses or Mohammed, but really was divine. On the other hand, if Jesus was divine, he could not have suffered as ordinary humans do—either physically or mentally. Hence, either the doctrine of the Incarnation is false or the Doctrine of the Atonement is false.

Our second theme in this chapter concerned differences created by Paul between the original ideas of Jesus and those of Paul's new revelations on the road to Damascus. In many ways, Paul was the first to try to think himself through the philosophical implications of making the message of Jesus acceptable to Hellenes. In so doing, Paul adopted his Gentile Mission and wrote in Greek. Others like him, including some of those who wrote the Gospels, followed his lead. Thus Paul's Christianity emerges as a partial melding of Judaism and Hellenism.

4

Mohammed and the Islamic Conception of God

▼ ▼ ▼

In this chapter we discuss a philosophical dilemma that arises from considering some qualities of the concept of Allah in Islam. Three introductory sections sketch Mohammed's founding of Islam, the pre-Islamic conception of God in Judaism, and the Islamic rejection of the Christian idea of a god-who-became-flesh. Then we discuss a dilemma about the concept of God in Islam concerning his human and impersonal qualities. Our discussion of the concept of the deity within world religions continues in the following chapter, which develops the idea of Brahman in Indian religions and contrasts it with the idea of Allah in Islam.

THE FOUNDING OF ISLAM

As one of the most influential people in recorded history, Mohammed (also transliterated as "Muhammad") is a very popular subject of biographers. According to the *Saint James Guide to Biography*, one bibliography ending in 1965 records over 1,500 titles devoted to him.[40] Since

---

[40] *Saint James Guide to Biography* (Chicago: Saint James Publishers, 1992), p. 541. For a detailed discussion of these problems, see Michael Cook's *Muhammed* (New York: Oxford University Press, 1983), chap. 7.

then, and also owing to the recent rise of influence of Islam in the world, many other biographers have written about Mohammed. It is perhaps no surprise that many of these biographies do not agree on key details. As for any founder of any ancient religion, it is often very difficult to be certain of many claims about Mohammed or his original views. Nevertheless, we can with some assurance believe the general facts recorded in the following account.

Mohammed was born in the late sixth century CE and died in 632. An only child, both his parents were dead by the time he was six, and he was raised by the family of his uncle, Abu Talib. Mohammed grew up in Mecca, a barren place among rocky hills, whose only resource was a religious shrine known as the Kabba (the black cube venerated by Muslims today who make the *hijira* or pilgrimage to it).[41] Because pilgrims came there, Mecca gradually became a center of trade in which a few wealthy men dominated.

Mohammed was undoubtedly a genius. He seems to have been an astute trader when he accompanied his uncle on trading journeys. Because he was an orphan with no real family and had inherited nothing, he could not fund his own caravan, which was the chief way in his time of making real money.

When he was twenty-five, Khadijah, a wealthy widow in her forties, hired Mohammed as her steward for a caravan from Mecca to Syria. Returning with success, Khadijah offered to marry him, which Mohammed accepted. They had six children, of which only four daughters survived to adulthood. Nothing at the time indicated that Mohammed would soon be one of the great founders of religion: "He was thus, at this stage, a somewhat marginal figure, who owed such success as he had achieved as much to his older and richer wife as to his own position in society."[42]

A custom of his time was to spend one month each year in a retreat, and while doing so on Mount Hira, the angel Gabriel came to Mohammed in a dream and ordered him: "Recite!" At first, Mohammed told his family, he disbelieved his dream, but after a while and with

---

[41] "Mohammed," in Montgomery Watt, *Encyclopedia of Religion*, (1987), p. 137–39.
[42] Cook, op. cit., p. 15.

help from his wife, he came to accept his calling to be the Messenger of Allah.

This process took a long time. As one commentator describes it,

> The desert *jinn* [spirits] were irrelevant to this quest, but one deity was not. Named *Allah*, he was worshipped by the Meccans not as the only God but as an impressive one nonetheless. Creator, supreme provider, and determiner of human destiny, he was capable of inspiring authentic religious feeling and genuine devotion. Certain contemplatives of the time, called *hanifs*, worshipped *Allah* exclusively, and Mohammed was one of their number. Through vigils, often lasting the entire night, *Allah*'s reality became for Mohammed increasingly evident and awesome. Fearful and wonderful, real as life, real as death, real as the universe he had ordained, *Allah* (Mohammed was convinced) was far greater than his countrymen supposed. This God, whose majesty overflowed a desert cave to fill all heaven and earth, was surely not a god or even the greatest of gods. He was what his name literally proclaimed: He was *the* God, One and only, One without rival. Soon from this mountain cave was to sound the greatest phrase of the Arabic language: the deep, electrifying cry that was to rally a people and explode their power to the limits of the known world: *La ilaha illa 'llah!* There is no god but God![43]

Mohammed's first revelations were received sympathetically by those who, like his wife Khadijah, were excluded from the powerful trading elite of Mecca. Mohammed emphasized that Allah was omnipotent, benevolent, and that humans must be generous and fair with their wealth. If people were not, at the Last Judgment they would be assigned to Hell.[44]

Mohammed's messages gradually found acceptance by others in Mecca, much to the ire of the elite Meccan merchants. Tensions increased and, were it not for the protection of his uncle's Quraysh

---

[43] Houston Smith, *The World's Religions*, rev. ed. (San Francisco: Harper, 1991), p. 225.

[44] "The great merchants thought they could control everything because of their wealth and expertise and that they could flout traditional nomadic moral standards with impunity, especially in such matters as the use of their wealth. It was therefore salutary for them to be told that, ultimately, events were controlled by God and that there was a future life in which their prospects would depend on their conduct in this present life. Thus there was a sense in which the revealed messages were directed against the powerful merchants who were the effective rulers of Mecca" (Watt, op. cit., p. 138).

tribe and its dedication to the clan's most basic rule of a-life-for-a-life retaliation, Mohammed might have been killed. Even then, many of his followers for three years went to Abyssinia (roughly today's Ethiopia), where they were warmly received and where they established trading partnerships.

In 619 CE, Abu Talib died, leaving Mohammed without a powerful protector in his clan. In such a precarious position, Mohammed sought out other cities where he could establish a seat of power. About 250 miles north of Mecca lies Medina, whose two chief clans with their respective Jewish allies had been fighting each other with devastating, unprofitable results just before Mohammed's visit. Unlike Mecca, there was no reason for Medina to be impoverished because it was a rich agricultural oasis. (The warring situation there resembles that of Bosnia today.) Yet no internal ruler could establish order without incurring the wrath of the other clans.

Mohammed's new message—of a religion where all clans had to submit (*Muslim* means "one who submits") to the will of Allah—was ideal for such a situation. Mohammed was seen as a divinely sent sovereign who could pull the warring clans out of a brutish state of nature into a mutually profitable civil order. In addition to the divine right that Mohammed claimed, it was also fortunate that his message was reasonable for the times—there was just one god, Allah, who was just and fair, and who expected his created beings to be likewise. He was a God who did not favor any particular tribe or clan, but ruled all Arabs impartially (the idea that all members of these clans had a common identity would not come until much later). Moreover, Allah's definition of fair was what a merchant could accept—a tithe on his profits for the poor, but not a complete ban on profits.

The merchants of Medina thus swore an oath to follow Mohammed and to protect him in battle. This oath, and a natural rivalry among cities for trading routes, led the leaders of Mecca to fear the new Prophet. This fear was justified because over the next several years, Mohammed led raiding parties against various Meccan caravans.

Finally, the Meccans organized a great campaign of ten thousand soldiers against Mohammed in 627, and at the Battle of the Trench (where Mohammed's men dug a deep trench around Medina), Mohammed resisted a siege and broke the alliance against him. About a year later, Mohammed arranged to enter Mecca under sanctuary of a pilgrimage to the Kabba, and soon thereafter his forces gained control of the city.

Although not every Meccan converted to Islam, a subsequent external threat proved convenient in uniting the Medinans and Meccans against a common enemy, whom they vanquished. Mohammed then used marriage to achieve political unity among previously warring clans (Mohammed had as many as fourteen wives, each of whom had a separate room in his quarters). Through such intermarriage and through military victory, Mohammed by 629 became chief of many clans: "There was now no Arab leader capable of raising a force that could meet Mohammed in battle. During the remaining two and half years of his life many, probably the majority, of the nomadic tribes throughout Arabia entered into his confederacy and accepted Islam. This was now a vast political unit, and much of Mohammed's time was devoted to ordering its affairs."[45]

It is of special interest to Westerners interested in separation of church and state to note that Mohammed worked from the beginning to establish a community where mosque and civil government were deeply intertwined on the most daily matters. This community had detailed rules for the conduct of war against external allies and for the eradication of internal blood-feuds. Unlike Jesus, Mohammed left a detailed system for almsgiving and a welfare system to take care of the poor. He made giving to charity one of the official duties of a Muslim and one of the five so-called pillars of Islam. Later, his teachings resulted in the *zakat*, a special tax on property for the poor.

Mohammed was constantly moving the clans toward a goal of political unity that paralleled their theological unity. These two concepts reinforced each other and were woven together into a seamless fabric: one God, one faith, one Muslim world, one political order, one last Prophet.

Mohammed died in his mid-sixties in 632. He named no successor, but had named Abu Bakr as his *caliph* or "deputy" in leading prayers

---

[45] Watt, op. cit., p. 152.

(normally led by Mohammed himself) when he had become ill. Abu Bakr's caliphate soon increased in power. Mohammed's cousin and son-in-law, Ali, was not named caliph on three different occasions but was finally so appointed, only to be assassinated. A minority of Muslims today called Shi'a or Shi'ites follow his branch of Islam and celebrate the death on the plains of Karbala of another Shi'a martyr, Hussein, a son of Ali, at their greatest festival.[46] (Incidentally, most Shi'a today are Persian, not Arab.) The overwhelming majority of Moslems today are Sunnis, "followers of the traditional path," Moslems who follow the conventions and traditions of the consensus of the Islamic community.

THERE IS NO GOD BUT ALLAH

According to the Koran (also transliterated as "Quran"), Abraham was neither Jew nor anything else but a simple *hanif*, a simple worshipper of the One God.[47] According to the Koran, Abraham's God was the same as that of Mohammed's two thousand years later.

In its most ancient conception, the Koran sees God as a king who sends messengers to earth. Mohammed was the greatest and last, but still just one prophet among others, such as Moses and Jesus. Implicit in this concept is the idea that the Divine sends different kinds of messengers to different kinds of people at different times in history. Most often, the people have been disobedient to what the Divine

---

[46] Since these Muslims celebrate a warrior hero's death, and when so celebrating act as if they were there with him on the fields of Karbala, one would think that they would not be a good group to pick as an enemy. Yet when Israel invaded southern Lebanon to pursue and expel the PLO in 1982, it stayed in these valleys and occupied the land of the southern Lebanese Shi'a (who have previously welcomed them as liberators). Israel (and its ally, the United States) thus made into enemies a people whose ties to Islam celebrate death by martyrdom. For more on this, see Thomas Freidman's Pulitizer-prize winning *From Beirut to Jerusalem* (New York: Farrar Straus and Giroux, 1989). See also the documentary, *Sword of Islam*, produced by Granada Films (London: 1985).

[47] Watt, op. cit., p. 142. Both Muslims and Jews trace their ancestry back to Abraham; Jews through Isaac and Arabs through Sarah's "handmaiden" Hagar, the "surrogate mother" of Ishmael with Abraham, and hence the pejorative name of Christians for Muslims, "Saracens," which is literally, "empty of Sarah."

requires and the messenger must admonish the people toward correct behavior.[48]

Mohammed emphasizes that, all along in history, there has been a primordial core conception of God which previous men in their ignorance and superstition either misunderstood or willfully disregarded. The Koran reveals the true concept of God as Allah to any one who submits.[49]

Does this mean that Islam endorses the modern idea of "many paths to the godhead" with many messengers in many different cultures and times? The answer is yes and no. Jews and Christians are "peoples of the book" who worship Allah under a different name, but other religions (especially those of the East) are heresies.

The bold idea in Islam is that Allah has existed from eternity and has, all along, been sending out the same message to humans of his simple, one nature and his simple requirements for (largely disobedient) humans. So the Koran makes Abraham not the founder of Judaism but the original monotheist. It was Abraham who had the genius to see that the God who spoke to him in Israel was with him all along in his journey from Ur (possibly near modern Kuwait). It was this same God whom the prophets referred to as "the God of our Fathers."

In later Islam, the notion becomes powerful that the world has been corrupted and hence that we cannot see the obvious existence of God or follow his commands. What is thus needed is a return to the simple purity of earlier times. This conservative idea of how to accomplish worldly reform has been a powerful idea in history. Traditional cultures regulate the present by the past, and appeals to reform often mean reviving models of behavior from a past perceived to be more pure. Such thinking is seen in the ideas of a pure, primitive Christian community, of the American Shaker communities, of Rousseau's "noble savage," of Native American peoples possessing a

---

[48] Here is another reason, not much discussed in the literature, why the ordinary person associates morality with God, i.e., most often the founder of a religion comes to sermonize and urge his people to live by a truer, higher standard.

[49] See Albert Hourani, *Islam in European Thought* (New York: Cambridge University Press, 1991), p. 15.

higher morality with great spirituality, and in the work of Cromwell's men in England in smashing what they saw as the corrupting, idolatrous images in papist churches.

In Islam, reform movements periodically arise, such as the Wahhabi movement of the eighteenth century. These movements emphasize *tajdid* ("renewal") and *islah* ("reform"). In these periodic movements, imams urge the faithful to return to the original, pure ways of Mohammed's teachings.[50]

It is worth noting here that Islamic societies today appear to some to be like Christian societies of centuries ago, and some people express the hope that these societies are merely a primitive stage of enlightened Christian tolerance—into which, they hope, Islamic society will one day evolve. That view might be a mistake. As we saw in chapter 2, Jesus left neither detailed writings about how to administer a practical morality nor a plan for establishing an organized religion (that was left to Paul). As such, it might have been easier for the Western governments to go their own way from the teachings of their founder than in Islam. It is certainly easy today in modern Western democracies, where we assume separation of church and state. But Mohammed did in fact leave detailed instructions for Islamic society, and his plan consciously bound mosque and state together. Where a Christian can read Jesus and find salvation outside the church, a Moslem needs Islamic society. As such, and in so far as it remains Moslem, Islamic society will not evolve into Western ideals, and it is a misunderstanding to believe that it will or should.

---

[50] "From its earliest days, Islam possessed a tradition of renewal and reform. Muslims had been quick to respond to what they regarded as the compromising of faith and practice; Kharijite secession, Shi'i revolts, the development of Islamic law, and Sufism. In succeeding centuries, a rich revivalist tradition expressed itself in a variety of concepts and beliefs.... The concepts of renewal (*tajdid*) and reform (*islah*) are fundamental component's of Islam's worldview, rooted in the Quran and the Sunna of the Prophet" (John L. Esposito, *Islam: The Straight Path*, 2nd edition. New York: Oxford University Press, 1991, p. 115). See also John O. Voll, "Renewal and Reform in Islamic History: Tajdid and Islah," chap. 2 of *Voices of Resurgent Islam*, ed. John L. Esposito (New York: Oxford University Press, 1983).

The Islamic Rejection of the Christian Incarnation

Arising in the sixth century CE, Islam had to distinguish its conception of Allah not only from YHWH of Judaism but also the Trinity of Christianity. It did so by vigorously denying that Allah ever became flesh or suffered as a man.

As discussed in chapter 3, early Christianity asserted that God had become flesh and blood, but this notion created many controversies. Within Christianity, the problem of the divine and human natures of Jesus was solved finally by the Council of Chalcedon in 451 CE, which promulgated that he was both human and divine. (A previous battle about the Trinity had been similarly "solved" at the Council of Nicea in 325 CE, which created the famous Nicene Creed that deals with the nature of God and other articles of faith.)

However, these councils and their conclusions never really solved the philosophical problems, and the peoples east of Constantinople and south of Jerusalem had special trouble accepting the Incarnation. Most of these peoples accepted a single-nature view of Jesus, and as such were called Monophysites (Christians believing in "one nature"). Some of these people were the Egyptian Copts, the Ethiopians, and the Syrian Jacobites. Some of them gained power and became small churches. During and after the fourth century CE, they thrived around the Mediterranean Sea. Some Christian bishops tried to ram the Chalcedonian Creed down the throats of these Monophysites, all of whom firmly rejected the dual nature of Jesus.

There they stayed, far away from the official Christian church. Thus such peoples—from the mountains of East Turkey to the southern tip of the Arabian peninsula, from the villages along the Nile to the deserts of Ethiopia—were ripe two centuries later for the monotheistic message of Mohammed:

> Most of the Christian churches [in the areas conquered by Mohammed of Iraq, Syria, Palestine, Persia, and Egypt] such as the Nestorians, Monophysites, Jacobites, and Copts had been persecuted as heretics

and schismatics by Christian orthodoxy. For these reasons, some Jewish and Christian communities aided the invading armies, regarding them as less oppressive than their imperial masters.[51]

According to Mohammed's Doctrine of Substitution in the Koran, God looked down and could not bear the suffering of his prophet, Jesus, so he sent down a likeness of Jesus and took the prophet up to Heaven. The Doctrine of Substitution says God substituted another man for Jesus, or a likeness of Jesus, but in neither case did Jesus or Allah die on the cross. This last point was always pressed by Muslims, who would ask Christians, "If Jesus was God, who saved Jesus on the cross and who resurrected him?" More substantially, how can an omnipotent God die?

Mohammed claimed that Christians were mistaken in believing that Jesus was God; instead, Jesus was merely a great prophet:

O People of the Scripture! Do not exaggerate in your religion nor utter aught concerning Allah save the truth. The Messiah, Jesus son of Mary, was only a messenger of Allah, and His word which He conveyed to Mary, and a spirit from him. So believe in Allah and His messengers, and say not "Three"—Cease! (It is) better for you!—Allah is only One God. Far is it removed from his transcendent majesty that he should have a son. (4.71)

They surely disbelieve who say: Lo! Allah is the third of three; where there is no God save the One God. If they desist not from so saying a painful doom will fall on those of them who disbelieve. (5.73)

Christians say that Jesus had to suffer to earn atonement for human sins. To Muslims, this was puzzling. Why is atonement needed in the first place? Allah himself forgives sin, without the intervention of Jesus. Muslims think that the philosophical web of ideas involved in accepting both the Incarnation and the atonement was unnecessary, contradictory, and beneath the dignity of Allah. Allah is Allah, they

---

[51] John L. Esposito, *Islam: The Straight Path*, expanded ed. (New York: Oxford University Press, 1991), p. 36.

assert. He did not need to become human to forgive sins and so he never in fact became flesh. What is his gain in so doing? It is beneath him to become human. If he wants to communicate with humans, he can send a messenger, such as Isaiah, Moses, Jesus, or his last, Mohammed.

ORIGINS OF THE CONCEPT OF ALLAH

In Islam, a tension exists between two ways of seeing God. The remainder of this chapter, and some of the next, explores this tension. On one hand, Allah acts in human ways, for example, as a king, and as such, has anthropomorphic qualities. On the other hand, Allah is incomprehensible and superhuman. Like the Arabian desert, Allah's great power covers such a huge territory that he is impossible to comprehend. Like this same desert, Allah moves in mysterious ways that do not always, or even usually, accommodate the wishes of the sojourner. Like this desert, Allah has the power to eradicate all human accomplishments and reduce them to nothing, if it is his wish to do so.

In the Koran, Mohammed says that Allah is the only God, and that he is Good, and Omnipotent:

> In the name of Allah, the Beneficent, the Merciful.
> 1. All that is in the heavens and all that is in the earth glorifieth Allah: unto Him belongeth sovereignty and unto Him belongeth praise, and he is Able to do all things.
> 2. He it is Who created you, but one of you is a disbeliever and one of you is a believer, and Allah is Seer of what ye do.
> 3. He created the heavens and the earth with truth, and He shaped you and made good your shapes, and unto Him is the journeying.
> 4. He knoweth all that is in the heavens and all that is in the earth, and He knoweth what ye conceal and what ye publish. Allah is Aware of what is in the breasts of men.
>
> . . .
>
> 11. No calamity befalleth save by Allah's leave. And whosoever

believeth in Allah, He guideth his heart. And Allah is the Knower of all things.[52]

This Koranic conception of Allah has a pedigree that began two thousands years before in Judaism. The most mysterious reference to any god in the Bible is in Exodus 6.2–3 where the Hebrew is El Shaddai, probably a mountainous storm god, who contrasted with the more passive, agricultural goddesses, such as Astarte, whose fertility rites guaranteed good harvests to farmers.[53] El Shaddai ruled the area around Mount Sinai and, later, the territory coextensive with the land of the Hebrews/Israelites. General Deborah calls on this God to come down from Sinai to the plains to help her people during an upcoming battle (Judges 5.1–12).

El Shaddai is not only a storm god but also a warlord. He ruthlessly aids the friends of the Hebrews and smites their enemies ("For mine Angel shall go before thee, and bring thee in unto the Amorites, and the Hittites, and Perizzites, and the Canaanites, and the Hivites, and the Jebusites, and I will cut them off" [Exodus 23.23]). When he changes into YHWH in the Tanak, the anthropomorphism of the conception gets the editors into trouble. So YHWH "walks" like a man in the Garden of Eden, "wrestles" with Moses and tries "to kill him" (Exodus 4.24), refuses to allow Moses to see his "face" on Mount Sinai but allows Moses to hear his "voice" and to see "his back" as he leaves. In Job, God "sits" on a throne and conversationally chats with Satan.

These are loose descriptions, perhaps metaphors, from very ancient writings. Some would say they merely show the aspirations and conceptions of a primitive people in their first thoughts about God. But the problem to Moslems is that some people take such anthropomorphic images literally and infer that Allah really is something like a very big human being or a very powerful king as "Lord of lords."

[52] All references to the Koran are to *The Glorious Koran*, trans. Marmaduke Pickthall (New York: Dorset Press, 1982). References to surah and verse therein are given in the text, e.g., the above quotation is from surah 64.1–4, 11.

[53] In the King James Version, this is translated as "God Almighty," which is rendered this way to make it similar to YHWH, the name of God used by the Israelites when Moses led them out of Egypt around 1500 BCE.

That is blasphemy to Muslims because it greatly insults and demeans the majesty of Allah.

In so vigorously denying that Allah became flesh, Islam at times seems to go to extremes in denying that God is in any way human. One of the great attractions to many Christian believers is a human face of a god, but it is precisely this human kind of "face" that is banned in Islam. In Islamic mosques, there are no pictorial representations of Allah at all, and it is considered sacrilegious to so picture Allah. The pictures familiar to many Christians, of a bleeding Jesus on the cross or a weeping, sorrowful Mary, are scorned by Muslims as heretical worship of mere humans.

To Muslims, early Judaism also demeans the concept of Allah by limiting his power to one geographical place. In Judaism, YHWH was "freed" from his temple in Jerusalem when the Jews left Jerusalem in various ways and the temple was destroyed. In exile, great Jewish thinkers came to believe that YHWH would come to any Jew who was pure.[54] This universalizing process continues in Islam. Once the purity of faith or submission could make God hear the prayer of the believer, it did matter if the sojourner was in a mosque or in the middle of the vast Sahara Desert. The power of Allah was not limited by place.

Perhaps the next most important change in the conception of YHWH before Islam came during the second exile of the Jews, when prophets such as Nathan and Elijah changed YHWH from an amoral warlord to a just king. As such, the prophets said, YHWH dictates not only to man, but also to kings. Moral virtues are human traits, but in Ezekiel, we also see the other part of the Islamic conception, that is, God as a transcendent, cosmic Other—a deity of unsurpassable mystery and power (Ezekiel 15). Second Isaiah emphasizes the unitary nature of YHWH as the one, high God.[55] In this defiant, confident

---

[54] Johnson, op. cit., chap. 1.

[55] "[Isaiah] asserted the absolute sovereignty of YHWH, his sole existence, and the nothingness of all other deities, with an explicit, sustained, uncompromising monotheism never hitherto found among the Hebrews. YHWH, as the Great Isaiah understood him, could say, "Before me there was no God formed, neither shall there be after me" (43.10), "I am the first, and am the last; and besides me there is no God" (44.6); "My hand hath laid the foundation of the earth, and my right hand hath spread out the heavens: when I call unto them, they stand up together"

monotheism, we see the core of Mohammed's later conception of Allah and his recurring, adamant theme that "there is no God but Allah."

In Islam, we are told repeatedly that at the conceptual heart of Islam is the majestic glory of Allah. Five times a day, the devout Muslim says, "I witness that there is no god but the God [Allah]." Allah, literally, "The God," is named more than 2,500 times in the Koran. He is described as transcendent, all-knowing, Creator, Sustainer, Ordainer, and Judge of humanity.

Yet Allah still has his human qualities. The Koran says Allah should be praised (e.g., 54.6; 103.6), that every Muslim must submit to Allah's will, that Allah will be the Judge who sends each man to heaven or hell at the Last Assembly, but that Allah is also "merciful" and "forgiving." Allah is often angry at humanity, which repeatedly disobeys his Laws. At the Last Judgment, Allah will retaliate against those who so disobey and make them burn for eternity in the fires of Hell.

So, on one hand, one basic Koranic picture of Allah is of an extremely powerful, human king who rules with absolute power over a vast domain. This picture in many ways has more in common with El Shaddai or YHWH than the loving "our Father who art in heaven" of the synoptic Gospels or the "Word" (*logos*) of the Gospel of John. As Creator, Judge, and Lawgiver to humans, Allah demands submission and obedience to his rules. But on a less human scale, Allah is also Lord, Master, and Absolute Ruler of the universe. His authority is unquestionable; his eye is all-seeing, and his wisdom is incomprehensible to mortals.

It is worth noting here a difference between Islam and Christianity in how each conceives the essential relationship between a human and the deity. For Christianity, the essential act is repentance, which

---

(48.13); and, as for other gods, they are "of nothing" and their "work is of nought" (41.24). Whether in his positive assertion of the one universal God . . . or in his scorn of all competitors, whom he placed in the category of worthless idols . . . he "held monotheism with all his mind," . . . and treated the gods of the nations "as things, in whose existence no reasonable person can possibly believe" (Harry Emerson Fosdick, *A Guide to Understanding the Bible*, [New York: MacMillan, 1920], p. 29). The quotation from Smith is listed by Fosdick as *The Book of Isaiah*, vol. 2, p. 40. This section owes a debt to the first chapter of Fosdick's work, "The Idea of God."

allows one to be "born again," get right with God, and receive salvation. For Islam, the essential act is submission, which allows one to fall under Allah's protection and to merit salvation in an afterlife. In later Christianity, a dispute emerges in the works of Martin Luther as to whether one is saved through works or through Grace. To believe that one can be saved through one's own efforts is to upgrade the status of humans and to weaken their total dependence on God for salvation. To believe that we are only saved through God's Grace is to render us totally dependent on his forgiveness and to make useless any amount of our good works. As such, the line of thought in Christianity emphasizing salvation only through Grace resembles a similar line of thought in Islam.

TENSIONS IN MOHAMMED'S CONCEPTION OF ALLAH

At times, the Koran increases Allah's powers so much that there seems to be little dignity left in being human. Just as Paul tended to denigrate humans and their unworthiness before God, so the Koran makes Allah so supreme and so mighty that the gulf between Allah and humans seems uncrossable. When the Koranic picture then emphasizes the omnipotence and omniscience of Allah—when it emphasizes the impersonal conception of the deity—it gives Islam its bent toward fatalism.

Fatalism is not determinism. Determinism is the doctrine that every event has a cause. This doctrine may or may not contradict the human belief in free will. One well-known view, compatibilism, asserts that determinism and free will are not contradictory but compatible. Fatalism, in contrast, is a much bleaker notion that renders human desires and choices impotent. It is an incompatibilist view, meaning here that free will is incompatible with a preordained universe.

Fatalism says that despite Oedipus's desire not to kill his father and not to commit incest with his mother—despite his flight from his land for years on his journeys around the world—he was powerless to change his fate:

> *The Moving Finger writes, and having writ,*
> *Moves on: nor all thy Piety nor Wit*
> *Shall lure it back to cancel half a Line,*
> *Nor all thy Tears wash out a Word of it.*[56]

The Calvinistic doctrine of predestination is fatalistic. For John Calvin, God preordained who will be saved and who will not, and if one is not saved, no amount of faith, good works, or effort will change this fact.

The Koranic conception of God does not shy away from fatalism: "No calamity befalleth save by Allah's leave" (64.11). Not a leaf falls without his knowledge, and his having willed the leaf's falling is part of his mighty plan. Nor does it limit God's omnipotence in any way—when Allah wants a new galaxy to exist, he has only to say, "Exist!" and it is instantly done.

One problem here, traditionally called the problem of foreknowledge, is that the following two statements seem contradictory: (1) Allah knows what will occur in the future; and (2) I am free to decide how I will act in the future. Having free will seems to require that my future be indeterminate; it seems to require that there are important choices left open to me. If I cannot help but choose wicked actions, such that I will not be saved, how can I deserve to go to Hell?

Moreover, if in fact I will choose the evil path and cannot be saved, then Allah certainly knows this fact. Allah knows everything about me and my future. If Allah already knows I will not be saved, then I am not really free to choose to submit to Allah. Augustine, in the fourth century CE, famously argued that God's knowledge of how in fact I will act in the future does not in itself compel me to act. I still act freely; it is just that God knows how I will choose when I later choose freely.

This compatibilist position of Augustine's, which many commentators believe does not work, is not the Islamic position, which is closer to Calvin's. In Islam, the gulf between man and God is vast, like the vast expanse of the Arabian desert. Just as it is not important to the

---

[56] *Rubaiyat of Omar Khayyam*, trans. Edward Fitzgerald (New York: Thomas Crowell, 1964), verse 50, p. 24.

desert whether any grain of sand believes itself to be free, so it is not to Allah whether any human believes himself or herself to have free will. What is, is.

The Koran, moreover, even more relentlessly than Calvin, emphasizes how lowly and insignificant we humans are. The Koran emphasizes not only that Allah knows everything in advance, but also that he causes everything to happen. It is by emphasizing this conjunction of Allah's omniscience and his omnipotence that the Islamic universe seems so resolutely fatalistic. If Allah causes everything, what is there left for humans to do? "Allah chooseth for Himself whom He will, and guideth unto Himself him who turned (toward Him)" (Koran 42.13). This is very close to Paul's discussion of God's Grace toward those who are already saved (in his letter to the Romans).

In contrast to Islam is the ancient (sixth-fifth century BCE) Persian religion of Zoroastrianism, which saw the universe as a cosmic struggle between the Lord of Light (Ahura Mazda) and the Lord of Darkness (Ahriman). Not only does each lord struggle for each person's soul, but each person determines his or her own fate by his or her allegiance to one side or the other—with the final outcome being determined by which God wins. In contrast, Islam—as a monotheistic religion with an infinitely powerful, all-knowing Allah—has no such titanic battle over the fate of the cosmos. In contrast, the individual Muslim has no role in the outcome of Islamic history.

Islam resolutely says Allah is a judge who may send us to Hell. But if we take seriously Allah's omniscience and omnipotence as the Koran urges us to do, why should we be sent to Hell for a life that Allah has ordained for us? What power do we puny mortals have to prevent it? If Allah has ordained our fate, what else can we do but accept it?

Consider a Christian who has recently been exposed to Islam and begins to realize that the great, grand conception of God as *Allah* in Islam is the true view. But the person cannot bring himself to announce to his fellow Christians that he believes that Islam is the true view. Privately, he prays to Allah to forgive him.

But we must ask why this Christian prays. What effect can his prayer have on Allah? Millions of years ago, Allah knew that this

Christian would be exposed to Islam (perhaps by reading this very chapter) and knew, too, that this Christian would waver in accepting his message. Whatever the final outcome—whether the Christian converts to Islam or backslides to Christianity—Allah knows all. Indeed, Allah not only knows all, he also creates all, sustains all, and ordains all:

> *With Earth's first clay They did the last man knead,*
> *And there of the Last Harvest sow'd the seed;*
> *Yea, the fist Morning of creation wrote,*
> *What the last Dawn of Reckoning shall read.*[57]

We can continue to scrutinize other characteristics of Allah's relation to us. Why should we ever ask Allah for forgiveness? The concept of forgiveness implies that in order to forgive someone, the one who might forgive must have been harmed or injured by the party who wants forgiveness. For example if a student has promised a paper to a professor by a certain time and asked the professor to stay late to receive it, then a student arriving after the requested time might consider asking for forgiveness. If the student arrives on time, the professor has not been harmed or injured and no thought arises on the student's part of asking for forgiveness.[58]

But Allah cannot be harmed or injured by any action done or not done by any human. Why therefore should any human ask for forgiveness? Nothing any individual human does can affect Allah. Indeed, nothing humanity has ever done or will ever do can effect Allah. No amount of conversions to belief, no amount of defections to atheism, can affect the mighty grandeur of the Self-sufficient Source. Certainly nothing we do can harm, injure, or affect Allah in any way that matters.

Moreover, and because of his omniscience, Allah is not only not injured by any belief or unbelief on our part, but also, he has known for millennia exactly what our belief or unbelief will be at each moment of our lives. It is certainly human hubris to think that

---

[57] Ibid., verse 53.
[58] On this topic, see Ann Minnas, "God and Forgiveness," in D. Shatz and S. Cahn, *Readings in Contemporary Philosophy of Religion* (New York: Oxford University Press, 1982).

whether or not I believe in Allah affects the universe, and it is even more arrogant to think that whether or not I believe actually affects Allah. Allah is great. Nothing about me can affect him.

Of course, the devout Muslim agrees. Allah in his majesty is not concerned to satisfy my lowly needs or even my desire to understand his nature. He does what he does, and that is that. But this side of the Islamic conception leads to a darker question.

If Allah is so impervious to human concerns, the question arises about how much Allah cares for humans. The problem of evil raises a similar issue (i.e., why does a benevolent, omnipotent God allow evil to occur?) From the evidence of the universe, it is sometimes difficult to infer that Allah really thinks humans are special.

Some say that the fact of his caring is shown because he sent messengers to us such as Moses and Mohammed. But what else can we infer from this? Because he has not sent a messenger in so long, can we then infer that Allah has stopped caring? Because he gave us three messengers and because we did not heed their call, should we infer that he has given up on us?

The Koran suggests that it is not for us to know. To Allah, we are as ants are to us. Our relation to insects is finite; our relation to Allah is of the finite to the infinite. Why indeed should he care about us? Omnipotent Allah has the power to make immortal one ant or all ants. From his view, why is that a good thing to do?

The Koran is not ignorant of these problems. Although Allah made humans, gave them rules to live by, and sent them prophets, why he does is not for us to know. It is even possible, the Koran sometimes hints darkly, that he does not care much for humans and views us like some haughty, disdainful king ruling over conquered subjects far away.

In contrast, modern Christianity emphasizes that God cares about humanity and, more important, that God really cares about me. In practice, ordinary Muslims today believe the same and do not accept every implication of the Koranic theology. In emphasizing the need for me to repent before God, Christianity implies that my real repentance is important. In emphasizing the requirement to submit daily before Allah, modern Islam implies that my real submission is important. (In any religion, what its ordinary adherents believe and what it teaches formally as theology can be worlds apart.)

But let us take one more step down the road of analyzing Allah's increasing powers, of "pumping up" his omnipotence. For example, the notion of wanting anything—for such a completely omnipotent being—seems absurd. Notions that supreme omnipotence needs our prayers, likes them, enjoys our praise, wants our hymn-singing, or becomes angry at those who do not follow the rules would seem to be holdovers from older, more primitive conceptions of God as a king who needs the loyalty of his subjects to rule.

Ultimately, if we increase Allah's omnipotence to infinity, we create such a vast gulf between Allah and us as to make the ordinary person begin to wonder if that gulf is not unbridgeable. Whether such a deity would really send messengers to earth to help us, whether such a deity would care a whit for humans, and whether he had any reason at all for creating humans (even on a whim, for it would indicate a limitation of his power to be subjected to whims), is all unknowable.[59]

In the next chapter, we explore this idea more by contrasting the Western conception of God-as-a-person with the Eastern conception of God (sometimes called "Brahman").

CONCLUSION

In this chapter, we discussed some background to the concept of Allah in Islam and saw how the Koran sketches a picture of Allah as a supremely powerful, but distant, sovereign. We also saw why some Muslims are troubled by how little room there appears to be in Islam for free will. We suggested that Islam's concept of an imperial, distant Allah has difficulty explaining why such a deity should care about humans or why humans have any role in history.

There is a possible antidote to this thought. The great nineteenth-century Christian philosopher, Søren Kierkegaard, emphasized that

---

[59] The notion of such a deity having a reason, in the sense of a justification or a plan, might also be an anthropomorphism.

the path of faith and the path of reason go in opposite directions at a crossroads.[60] Down the path of reason lies the demands of evidence, analysis, reason, and verification. Kierkegaard stressed that to go down that path is to give up on obtaining the special insights of the "leap of faith." To start out on the wrong path is to accept, at the very beginning, that one will not reach the true goal. When faced with such puzzles as those raised in this chapter, Augustine said famously, "Lord, let me believe, that I might understand."

The Koran agrees with this submissive attitude. It asserts that although its surahs reveal Allah's laws and will, they do not reveal Allah himself: "Vision comprehendeth Him not, but He comprehendeth (all) vision. He is the Subtile [subtle], the Aware" (6.103). So the devout Muslim might say, "Lord, let me submit, that I might accept."

---

[60] Søren Kierkegaard, *Fear and Trembling* (Princeton: Princeton University Press).

5

Is God a Person?

▼ ▼ ▼

Hinduism on Brahman

ALLAH AND BRAHMAN

In the eleventh century CE, the great Muslim scholar, Muhammad al-Biruni, wrote a history of India. In preparation for this work, he traveled widely in India and learned to read Sanskrit, the classical Indian language of scholarship and philosophy.

Al-Biruni developed a particular fascination with Indian religious thought (the tradition that we now call Hinduism), even translating several religious texts into Arabic and Persian. Despite his sympathetic interest and wide knowledge, he found little in common between his own Islamic faith and Indian religion. He wrote in his history: "The Hindus totally differ from us in religion, as we believe in nothing in which they believe and *vice versa*."[61]

Al-Biruni's comment is much too extreme if it is taken to apply to the full range of religious doctrines currently included under the label Hinduism. That label embraces a multitude of different sorts of religious outlooks, some of which are not that different from al-Biruni's own beliefs.[62] However, Hinduism also includes strands of

---

[61] This passage is quoted in R. C. Zaehner, *Hinduism* (New York: Oxford University Press: 1966) p. 4.
[62] See Zaehner, ibid., and T. W. Organ, *Hinduism: Its Historical Development* (Woodbury, N.Y.: Barran's Educational Series, 1974) for excellent discussions of the variety of religious views found within Hinduism.

religious thought that offer accounts of God and of our relationship to God and that differ dramatically from the conception of God usually associated with Islam (and with Judaism or Christianity). One such strand leads back to a body of ancient writings called the Upanishads. It is this tradition that al-Biruni had in mind when he made his comment, and, as we shall see in this chapter, his observation is very nearly correct.

To give the reader a preview of the upcoming discussion, we shall begin with a bold statement of the contrasts we will develop more fully over the course of the chapter. In Islam, as in Judaism and Christianity, God is conceived of as a person. Hereafter, purely for the sake of convenience, we shall call this the Western concept of God and we shall use the Arabic term *Allah* when we want to refer to God as conceived in the Western tradition. What is a person? Philosophers and theologians use this familiar word in a special sense. In this sense, "person" does not mean "human being." Rather, it means "a being capable of intentional action." Persons have reasons for doing what they do. They have purposes, goals, plans, and they act in order to accomplish their purposes or achieve their goals. Of course, human beings are persons in this sense. But, according to Western tradition, Allah is also a person.

The difference between us and Allah is that Allah is a perfect person. Our power to accomplish our purpose is limited; Allah's power is unlimited. If Allah wills something, it happens. Our purposes are sometimes evil and our actions are sometimes unjust. Allah wills only what is good and never does wrong. We are created by Allah and our well-being, our very existence, depends on Allah's will. Allah is in no way dependent on us, but even so, Allah offers us his love and protection with infinite mercy.

As God is conceived in the Upanishads, none of the above statements is true of God. The Sanskrit term in the Upanishads that refers to God is *Brahman*. Brahman is not a person. Brahman neither acts nor has any motive for action. Brahman simply exists: eternally serene, utterly secure, desiring nothing. We are driven by desires and aversions and are constantly insecure, always prey to uncertainty and frustration. Brahman will do nothing to save us from our unhappy condition; Brahman neither loves us, nor pities us, nor takes any interest in our suffering. But we can save ourselves. By putting aside all our attachments to life in this world, we can attain Brahman's peace and eternal serenity. Indeed, according to the Upanishads, we can become Brahman. All we need do is to surrender our personhood.

As al-Biruni suggests, these two conceptions of God have little in common. But not quite nothing in common. The Upanishads and the Western religions agree on at least one truth about God: "God is a perfect being." The differences between believers who think of Allah and those who think of God as Brahman arise ultimately from a fundamental disagreement about whether a perfect being could be a person. This is the issue we shall explore in our discussion of the Upanishads. But first, we need to tell the reader more about what the Upanishads have to say about Brahman and about human existence.

THE BACKGROUND OF THE UPANISHADS

The Vedas, a collection of hymns, incantations, and ritual instructions, contain the earliest written record of Indian religious thought.[63] They depict a pattern of religious beliefs and practices similar to ancient Middle Eastern and Greek polytheism. The natural world is ruled by various gods and goddesses (called *devas* in Sanskrit, the language of the Vedas). The devas are powerful, immortal beings whose lives are free from the worries that preoccupy humans. Human life, by contrast, is inherently uncertain. We are at the mercy of the forces of nature—cold, heat, flood, drought, and wind. We are prey to accidents, evil doing, disease, and old age. Our only certainty is death. Our security lies in service to the devas, whose favor we can win by prayer and sacrifices. Acceptable service brings us health, prosperity, and power. Neglecting or offending the gods invites calamity. The Vedas teach us how to serve. They enumerate the names and powers of the devas, show us how to praise them, and instruct us in the proper way of conducting rites and sacrifices. Certain verses in the Vedas

---

[63] See Organ, ibid., pp. 97–124, and Zaehner, op. cit., pp. 54–79, for an account of the Vedas.

even hold out the possibility that those who please the gods might be rewarded with life after death in a happy realm beyond this world.

The basic picture of reality in the Vedas was widely accepted in India by about 1000 BCE and remains a part of popular religion in India down to the present. (We should note that even in popular religion there have been many changes since 1000 BCE; for example, the gods currently worshipped are not the ones most prominent in the Vedas.)[64] However, we have evidence that by around the ninth century BCE, some Indian thinkers had begun to question the picture presented in the Vedas. This questioning reached a crescendo in the sixth to the fourth centuries BCE. During that time, several schools of thought totally rejected the Vedic conception of reality. Included in this *Nastika* (nay-saying) tradition were religious/philosophical movements such as Buddhism, Jainism, materialism, and fatalism.[65]

Other thinkers retained a respect for the Vedas, but argued that the Vedic account of reality should not be taken at face value. Since they affirm, at least in some respects, the truth of the Vedas, theirs is called the *Astika* (yea-saying) tradition. This tradition holds that the Vedas can be interpreted on many levels. The average believer can continue to take the Vedic picture literally, worshipping the various devas and relying on the Vedic rituals. Such believers will reap rewards appropriate to their level of spiritual development. But those possessed of greater intellectual curiosity, more imagination, and more intense spiritual hunger might discover a deeper level of reality. If you are willing to discipline yourself to rise above the distractions of day-to-day existence, to sharpen your intellect through rigorous argumentation and inquiry, to free your mind by meditation from preconceptions and ossified habits of thought, you might penetrate beneath the surface of the Vedas to the ultimate reality from which they spring. Some thinkers believed that they had succeeded in uncovering this reality. Some of these became *rishis* or *gurus*, that is, teachers who were prepared to help others discover for themselves these deeper truths.

Thus was born a religious literature known as the Upanishads. The

---

[64] Ibid., pp. 80–96.
[65] We discuss Buddhism in chapter 6. See Organ, ibid., for a discussion of the other traditions.

term *upanishad* means "sitting down together." It refers to the practice of the rishi gathering together a group of devoted students in a place where their conversation would not be overheard by the uninitiated. The teachings of the Upanishads were not meant for the causal listener, but only for those fully dedicated to the search for enlightenment.

The oldest of the Upanishads probably date from around 800 BCE. They consist of discourses, frequently in the form of questions and answers. Sometimes the Vedic gods appear as characters in the dialogues, but usually the participants are human beings. A great many Upanishads were written down, about two hundred, but only a few achieved wide influence. By about 300 BCE, the existing Upanishads had come to be regarded as *shruti*, that is, as sacred literature comparable in status to the Vedas themselves. About the authors of these writings, we know nothing of a personal nature, not even their names. They left us only the record of their teachings.[66]

THE WISDOM OF THE UPANISHADS

The Upanishads do not present a single, unified body of doctrine. Servepalli Radhakrishnan, a noted modern scholar, says of the Upanishads, "So numerous are their suggestions of truth, so various are their guesses at God, that almost anybody may seek in them what he wants and find what he seeks."[67] Nevertheless, they contain certain common themes, and a general picture, both of God and of our relation to God, does emerge from them. This picture is very different from anything suggested by a literal reading of the Vedas. The basic elements of this picture are the following:

Samsara.

Contrary to the literal interpretation of the Vedas, human beings are not allotted only one life in this world, to be followed, perhaps, by an afterlife in some otherworldly heaven or hell.

[66] See Organ, ibid., pp. 97–124, and Zaehner, op. cit., for an account of what is known about the Upanishads and their authors.
[67] S. Radhakrishnan, *Indian Philosophy*, vol. 1 (New York: MacMillan, 1923), p. 118.

In the Katha Upanishad, Nachiketa, a young man well-versed in the Vedas, visits Yama, the Lord of Death, sort of an Indian version of the grim reaper. He asks Yama to answer a question: "When a man dies, there is this doubt: some say he is; others say is not. Taught by thee, I would know the truth."[68] Yama first tries to palm Nachiketa off with the traditional story, even offering to teach him the fire sacrifice, which, performed properly, is supposed to guarantee reaching heaven. But Nachiketa refuses to accept this response. He persists, saying, "Tell me, O King, the supreme secret regarding which men doubt" (p. 15). Won over by Nachiketa's sincere desire for wisdom, Yama finally consents to reveal the secret. When you die, says Yama, your body falls away from you and goes on to destruction, but you, the person who inhabited this body, (the *jiva* or individual soul) do not cease to exist. Rather the jiva is reborn into the world, takes on another body, and lives out another life of pleasures and pains, hopes and fears, successes and failures in this world. That life ends in another death that is followed by another rebirth, another life, another death, and so on indefinitely into the future. We are caught, Yama says, on a great, ever-turning wheel of birth and death. *Samsara* is the name of this repeating cycle.

Karma.

What causes us to be reborn? Why should the jiva return to this world? We are drawn back into the world by the actions we performed and by the attachments that we formed in our previous life. In that life, we desired and pursued the things of this world. We sought the pleasures of bodily existence; we desired wealth and worldly success, we longed for the love and respect of other people, for power and influence over them; and we thirsted for knowledge of the world and the ability to manipulate it to our advantage. Such attachments to the world do not cease when the body dies. They remain in the jiva, demanding fulfillment, and pulling the jiva back into another body and into

---

[68] *The Upanishads*, trans. Swami Prabhavananda and Frederick Manchester (New York: New American Library: 1957), p. 15. All quotations from the Upanishads are taken from this edition.

another life in this world. *Karma* is the name of the universal law of cause and effect whereby the attachments formed in one life work themselves out in further lives.

Moksha.

Is there any end to this cycle? Can the jiva ever free itself from karma and escape the wheel of samsara? Yes. Yama explains to Nachiketa that, so long as one clings to the things of this world and makes such things the objects of one's desires and actions, "he falls again and again, birth after birth, into my jaws" (p. 17). But should one become indifferent to the things of this world, should one give up one's attachment to pleasure, health, wealth, status, power, life; and surrender one's fear of pain, sickness, poverty, contempt, death, then one will attain release from the wheel of samsara. This liberation from the round of births and deaths is called *moksha*.

The complex of doctrines—samsara, karma, moksha—outlined above are found not only in the Upanishads, but also in some of the *Nastika* traditions such as Buddhism and Jainism. Together they comprise an account of the human condition that strongly appealed to a wide variety of early Indian thinkers. These ideas are still current in those parts of the world that were influenced by Indian religious thought, for example, Japan, China, and Southeast Asia. Indeed, they have won many adherents in the Western world, despite their radical discontinuity with the account of the human condition in Judaism, Christianity, and Islam.[69]

So, the samsara-karma-moksha system is not distinctive of the Upanishads, though it might have had its first expression in them. What is distinctive about the picture in the Upanishads is its account of God and of how human beings are related to God. So far, we have said nothing about God, but we shall now proceed to do so.

---

[69] Though not incorporated into any of the Western religions, beliefs similar to the Upanishadic picture are found in Greek philosophy. For an example, see Plato's *Phaedo*, in *Five Dialogues*, trans. G. M. A. Grube (Indianapolis: Hackett Publishing, 1981).

Atman and Brahman.

One way to see the place of God in the Upanishads is to start with a question: Why should we desire to achieve moksha? What's so great about getting off the wheel of samsara? The idea that one might be reborn into the world after one's death (be "reincarnated") appeals to many people, especially in the West. The possibility seems to offer a chance for further adventures and experiences. Perhaps some of these further lives would be disagreeable, but others might be very reward-ing. Why should we want to forego the chance at these further lives? But the Upanishads clearly regard the prospect of continuing around on the wheel of samsara as something that it is worth all our efforts to avoid. Why so?

In the Katha Upanishad, Nachiketa rejects all the pleasures of life in this world. He even rejects the chance to continue such pleasures in a permanent heavenly world. His reason is that he has found that, even when he fulfills his worldly desires, satisfying his desires does not satisfy him. The great problem of life in this world is that, when our desires go unfulfilled, we suffer the torments of frustrated long-ing, but when they are fulfilled, that fulfillment (alas!) brings us no genuine peace or contentment.

Why should this be so? It's easy to see how frustrated desires could make our lives miserable, but why should getting what we want leave us unsatisfied? Because the objects of our worldly desires are not what we really want. Bodily pleasures, wealth, success are what we think we want. However, we are ignorant of our own true nature. I think of myself in terms of a particular physical body, and I see my own well-being as bound up with the care and feeding of that body. But I am not this body and ultimately what happens to it is of no consequence for me. I think of myself as living a particular life, in a particular set of circumstances, related to particular other persons. I see myself as a success or a failure according to what I accomplish in this life. But this is not my life. My existence extends far beyond the temporary events, circumstances, and achievements of this life, and ultimately, how it goes does not matter for me. I am not something limited and imper-manent. Therefore, no amount of limited, impermanent pleasures and successes will satisfy me. I want something perfect, complete, and eternal. I want something that speaks to what is perfect and eternal in me. I want an existence that is free of everything that is limited and imperfect. I want a god-like state of utter contentment, complete security, absolute self-sufficiency. I want, in fact, to be God.

Obviously a tall order. But, the remarkable secret of the Upanishads is that I can get what I want. I can be God. Indeed, I am God already, if I but knew it. In the Chandogya Upanishad, Svetaketu, who has sought enlightenment without success at the feet of many teachers, turns at last to his own father, Uddalaka. Uddalaka tells him that the wisdom he seeks consists in this:

> Truly has this universe come forth from Brahman. In Brahman it lives and has its being. Assuredly, all is Brahman . . . of all things he is the subtle essence. He is the truth. He is the Self. And that, Svetaketu, that art thou. (pp. 64, 69)

"That art thou" ("Tat tvam asi" in Sanskrit) represents the central teaching of the Upanishads. The underlying reality in each of us, that which persists through samsara taking on many forms but remaining always the same, is the *atman*. And this reality, this atman, is Brahman, the Lord of the universe. "He through whom man sees, tastes, smells, hears, feels, and enjoys is the omniscient Lord" (Katha Upanishad, p. 20). We, and all the other things in the universe, are manifestations of a single underlying reality. The constituents of the universe exhibit different forms and are called by different names. But what takes on those forms and is called by these names is the same in every case. It is Brahman. Brahman is the permanent, self-sufficient, perfect reality behind all the transitory, dependent, limited things of the world. Brahman is what is permanent and perfect within each of us.

But in our ignorance we mistake the particular form and activities that constitute our current existence for our true selves. I identify the atman, the reality in me, with a particular human life. I see myself as a body, separate and distinct from all other bodies. I see myself as a mind separate and distinct from all other minds. The Taittiriya Upanishad speaks of the atman as being covered or bound within sheaths, like the pith within the tightly wrapped leaves of a reed (p. 55). The sheaths represent the body, the thoughts and feelings, the habits and traits of character, and the sense of ego or individual self-consciousness that make up my personal life in this world. But these sheaths (the *koshas*) are not the atman. They are only the temporary, limited, imperfect forms that the atman has taken on in a particular life. In its own nature the atman can take on any form, but is ultimately beyond all forms. When the koshas have been peeled back, the *atman* stands forth as it really is, as something that transcends every limitation, as Brahman.

In order to achieve moksha then, we need only come to see ourselves as we really are. We need to identify ourselves not with what limits us and separates us from the rest of reality, but with the reality that is beyond all limitation. Thus Yama instructs Nachiketa:

> Man looks toward what is without, and sees not what is within. Rare is he who, longing for immortality, shuts his eyes to what is without and beholds the self. Fools follow the desires of the flesh and fall into the snare of all-encompassing death: but the wise, knowing the self as eternal, seek not the things that pass away. He through whom man sees, tastes, smells hears, feels, and enjoys is the omniscient Lord. He, verily, is the immortal Self. Knowing him, one knows all things. He through whom man experiences is the all-pervading self. Knowing him, one grieves no more. . . . What is within is also without. What is without is also within. He who sees difference between what is within and what is without goes evermore from death to death. By the purified mind alone is *Brahman* attained. *Brahman* alone is—nothing else is. He who sees the manifold universe, and not the one reality, goes evermore from death to death. (Katha Upanishad, pp. 20–21)

THE NATURE OF BRAHMAN

Before revealing to Nachiketa that the atman is identical with Brahman, Yama warns him: "Even the gods were puzzled by this mystery. Subtle indeed is the truth regarding it, not easy to understand" (Katha Upanishad, p. 16). Yama's warning is well justified. The doctrine that the atman is Brahman bristles with difficulties. How can I be or become Brahman? What exactly is Brahman anyway, and what would it be like to be Brahman? Later Indian thinkers expended great effort and subtlety in devising answers to these questions. We shall not attempt to review all their various answers. But we shall explore, very tentatively, some of the implications of this central teaching of the Upanishads.

Although we have said that Brahman represents my real self, the reality behind my various lives, it seems clear that achieving moksha, union with Brahman, is the end of my personal existence. If I peel back my koshas and you peel back yours, we shall find exactly the same thing, Brahman. What distinguishes you from me is your body, your thoughts and feelings, your particular sense of ego. What remains when these sheaths are discarded is the same for both of us. When I become one with Brahman, then, I lose everything that distinguishes me from other persons: and, indeed, from any other object in the universe (because everything is Brahman). Thus, attaining perfection, becoming God, means ceasing to be the particular person that I am:

> Individuality arises by identification of the self, through ignorance, with the elements; and with the disappearance of consciousness of the many ... it disappears. Where there is consciousness of Brahman, individuality is no more. (Brihadaranyaka Upanishad, p. 88.)

What sort of existence awaits me then? I shall become Brahman, but what is this thing called Brahman? Here it is difficult to find a clear answer in the Upanishads. Since, ultimately, everything is Brahman, every quality which belongs to anything is, in some sense, a characteristic of Brahman. Can we say anything about the nature of Brahman itself, apart from Brahman's manifestations in the universe of name and form? The Upanishads employ various metaphors in describing Brahman, comparing Brahman to the clay from which different kinds of vessels are made or to the ocean into which all streams eventually flow, but such analogies are not much help. Sometimes the Upanishads declare that Brahman's nature cannot be known.

> If you think that you know well the truth of Brahman know that you know little. What you think to be Brahman—that is not Brahman. The ignorant think that Brahman is known, the wise know him to be beyond knowledge. (Kena Upanishad, p. 31)

But this is even less help. Let's see if we can do better. It seems we can say at least that, if we were to see reality from Brahman's point of view, or, more accurately, if we see all reality as Brahman, then all the distinctions we draw among things would cease to have any importance. In our ordinary experience we divide things up into better and worse, beneficial and harmful, beautiful and ugly, good and evil. Such distinctions of value do not exist from Brahman's point of view. The Isha Upanishad says: "He who sees all things in the Self [i.e., Brahman] and the Self in all things, hates none. To the illumined soul, the Self is all. For him who sees everywhere oneness, how can there be delusion or grief?" (p. 27).

Since, for Brahman or in Brahman, there are no distinctions of value—nothing is better or worse than anything else—Brahman has no desires or aversions. Brahman loves nothing and hates nothing. "Brahman is passionless and indivisible" (Mundaka Upanishad, p. 46). Again and again, the Upanishads describe Brahman as utterly calm, unshakably serene, never moved by hope or fear, having no wishes and no plans. In a word, Brahman is "apathetic" (literally, "passionless").

Since Brahman never prefers anything to anything else, it follows that Brahman never acts. To act is to do something with some purpose in mind or, at least, to be moved by some motive or reason. Lacking all desire, Brahman can have no motive for action. Thus, Shankara (probably seventh century CE), perhaps the most acute interpreter of the Upanishads, proclaims that Brahman "neither acts nor is subject to any change"[70] and maintains that Brahman is "free from all attachment and [hence] beyond all action."[71] Though human beings, who

[70] Shankara, *The Crest-Jewel of Discrimination*, trans. Swami Prabhavananda and Christopher Isherwood (New York: New American Library: 1970) and reprinted in *Voices of Wisdom*, ed. G. E. Kessler (Belmont, Calif.: Wadsworth Publishing, 1992) p. 241. Shakara is a later Indian thinker. For an account of his views, see Organ, op. cit., pp. 241–69.
[71] Ibid., p. 243.

are only limited and incomplete manifestations of Brahman, do act and change, Brahman in its own nature remains unmoved. "To the ignorant the Self appears to move—yet it moves not" (Isha Upanishad, 27) or, as Shankara puts it, "It is false awareness alone that can explain the notion of [Brahman] as an agent."[72]

Does not Brahman create the universe? Not if by "creation" one means a deliberate action. In Western religions the universe is something distinct from Allah, brought into existence by Allah's will in accordance with Allah's purposes. In the Upanishads the universe is not distinct from Brahman and is not brought into existence by any act of will. It is simply a manifestation or expression of Brahman's being. The Mundaka Upanishad compares the universe coming forth from Brahman to various automatic, natural processes: "As plants grew from the soil and hair from the body of man, so springs the universe from the eternal Brahman" (p. 43). The metaphor should not be pushed too hard, but it does accurately convey the sense that creation is not something planned, desired, or willed by Brahman.

So, though perhaps we cannot say what Brahman is, we can say what Brahman is not. Brahman is not a person or an agent. Allah is an active, personal being. Allah is not indifferent to what happens in the universe. Allah loves righteousness and hates iniquity. Allah is moved by compassion for our suffering and anger at our disobedience. Allah wills and acts. Brahman, perfectly serene, is beyond will and action. Thus, in realizing my oneness with Brahman, I do not merely cease to be the person I am. Instead, I move entirely beyond personal existence. I became something which does not act, but simply is.

To readers whose ideas about God derive from the Western religions, this impersonal conception of God might seem strange and highly unsatisfactory. Many of those in the West have fled from Christianity and Judaism to seek greater fulfillment and spiritual growth in Eastern religions, such as Hinduism and Buddhism. However, our discussion here (and in the next chapter) indicates that they might not find what they seek. For a presupposition of most such

[72] *Encyclopedia of Indian Philosophy*, vol. 3, trans. K. H. Potter, (Princeton: Princeton University Press, 1981), p. 128.

Western seekers is that their ego or self will be transformed in some way if they obtain the goal of these Eastern religions. These seekers hope to be enlightened, awakened, or achieve some beatific vision of the divine. All of these typical expectations include the Western seeker's self being in the picture as the object transformed, fulfilled, or inspired. None of the visions include the disappearance of his or her ego. As such, for the rare few from the West who actually achieve the goals of Eastern religions, the results might feel neither ecstatic nor blissful, but traumatic.[73]

Indeed, the nonpersonal account of God has little appeal to most people who consider themselves Hindus. As the authors of the Upanishads knew full well, the typical believer will find little comfort in the prospect of union with Brahman. They recognized that the concept of God to which their meditations led them was very far from the picture of an active, loving protector cherished by most believers. "Brahman," says the Kena Upanishad, "is not the being who is worshipped by men" (p. 31). What can be said in defense of a nonpersonal conception of God?

Al-Biruni's statement to the contrary, Muslims and others who believe in a personal God do tend to share one belief about God with those who follow the teachings of the Upanishads: all agree that God is perfect. Now if God is perfect, then nothing could happen that would make God better off or improve God in any way. Shankara writes that, "It is of the nature of Brahman [that] no excellence can be added [to Brahman].[74] There is nothing that Brahman could do which would increase Brahman's excellence or would result in Brahman's being better than Brahman already is. So a perfect being could have, in itself, no motive for acting.

But could not a perfect being be motivated to do something for someone else? God might be perfect, but we are not. Couldn't God be moved to act in order to help us? According to the Upanishads, however, there is nothing that exists outside *Brahman*. All is Brahman;

---

[73] This is also the theme of E. M. Forster's novel *A Passage to India*. See also the discussion by Arthur Danto, *Mysticism and Morality* (New York: Harper Torchbook, 1975).
[74] *A Source Book in Indian Philosophy*, ed. S. Radhakrishnan and C. A. Moore (Princeton: Princeton University Press: 1957), p. 512.

we are Brahman. So there is no other to whom Brahman might render aid.

And why should there be anything existing which is distinct from God? Since God's existence in itself represents the pinnacle of perfection, a reality consisting of God plus a separate universe could be no more perfect than a reality consisting simply of God alone. Therefore, God can have no motive for creating anything distinct from God. So if a universe exists which is distinct from God, then that universe must exist on its own, independent of God's will. But this contradicts another belief about God that is generally held by those who regard God as a person, namely, the belief that God creates the universe and that everything in the universe depends for its existence on God's will.

Finally, one might object that, although God is perfect, God needs to act in order to remain perfect: that is, in order to prevent things from happening that would make God less excellent. On this view, God could not be more perfect than God already is, but God must act in order to preserve this perfect condition. But this objection seems to entail that things could happen which would make God worse off, that God's perfection is threatened, even if it is never actually compromised. A defender of the Upanishads' conception of God might plausibly argue that a being whose perfection is absolutely secure—a being which could not possibly become imperfect—is superior to a being whose perfection is threatened by possible further developments. Real perfection requires, not merely that God is perfect, but that no matter what happens, God could not possibly become less than perfect. Since Brahman is perfect, then, for Brahman, "there is nothing to be achieved or avoided."[75]

If they are sound, the above arguments show that a perfect being could have no motive for doing anything. By definition, to act is to do something with some motive or with some reason, so a perfect being cannot act. The whole point of being able to act is to be able to do things that will make things better for you in some way. If you were fortunate enough to be in such a condition that things could not

[75] Potter, op. cit., p. 151.

possibly be better for you than they are, then having a capacity for action would be of no use to you. But having the capacity to act, being an agent, is an essential part of being a person. Hence, it follows that a perfect being cannot be a person. Being a person is, by its very nature, an imperfect condition.

What can be said in favor of the Western idea that God is both perfect and a person? Obviously, people might find it comforting to believe that they are loved and protected by an omnipotent, omniscient, perfectly benevolent God. But there is more than wishful thinking behind the Western conception of God. One might argue that if we accept the claim that a perfect being cannot be an agent, we ought to also deny that a perfect being could be intelligent. Knowledge has value only in the context of action. We need to know because we need to choose. For a being who is utterly indifferent, who never makes decisions or initiates any action, knowledge would at best be useless. Having no reason to act, such a being would have no reason to know anything. Thus, one might charge that the Upanishadic conception of perfection leads to a picture of God as a being who not only lacks desires, but who also lacks any awareness of itself or the world. This is not a picture of something that is more than a person, but rather of something that is less than a person. It reduces God to the status of a thing.

The Upanishads do sometimes describe Brahman as having "neither senses nor mind" (Kaivalya Upanishad, p. 116). However, they generally insist that Brahman is conscious. Brahman is said to have (or sometimes, to be) "pure unitary consciousness." Such consciousness involves no awareness of distinctions, because all distinctions are illusory, and its contents cannot be described (Mundukya Upanishad, p. 51). In response to the charge that such a consciousness could be of no use to Brahman, the Upanishadic philosophers would reply that questions about the value of consciousness are beside the point. Consciousness is not something Brahman needs in order to obtain perfection. Rather, it is simply a part of Brahman's perfection.

But Western thinkers might say the same about agency. That is, they could claim that Allah's will is not something that Allah needs to have in order to accomplish some further purpose. Rather, being an agent is simply part of Allah's perfection. They could maintain that the very idea of a perfect being is the idea of an active, willing being. For them, being an agent or a person is part of what it means to be perfect.

CONCLUSION

We leave it to our readers to decide what they think about the arguments presented above. Our purpose has been to encourage the reader to reflect on the implications of the claim that God is perfect. Such reflection might lead the reader to choose one of the two interpretations of God's perfection over the other and, accordingly, either to worship Allah or to seek union with Brahman. Alternatively, such reflection might cause the reader to wonder whether it is really a good idea to say that God is perfect.

That God is perfect is the one point on which Western and Upanishadic traditions agree. But some theologians believe that the term "perfection" is too slippery and unclear to provide a useful description of God.[76] Perhaps, rather than argue about whether a perfect being can be a person, one should question whether God is a perfect being.

---

[76] C. Hartshorne, *Omnipotence and Other Theological Mistakes* (Albany: State University of New York Press, 1984) provides a good exposition of this view.

6
Does Anything Survive Death?
▼ ▼ ▼
What the Buddha Taught

In this chapter, we discuss the Buddha's seemingly contradictory views on whether a person can survive death. In what follows, we attempt to give the reader some guidance over this confusing philosophical terrain in Indian thought.

THE LIFE OF BUDDHA

Siddhattha Gotama sat down one evening under the spreading branches of a fig tree that grew on the bank of the River Neranjara near a place that would come to be called Buddha-Gaya. He had the strong premonition that his quest for enlightenment, to which he had devoted the previous six years of his life, was nearing its completion. He therefore made a vow that he would not arise from under this tree until he had achieved enlightenment. The tree would later be named the "Bodhi" or "Bo" tree (the tree of enlightenment) in honor of the event that had occurred beneath its branches.

Siddhattha had been born into a princely family thirty-five years before that evening. He grew up on a great estate in the cool foothills of the Himalaya Mountains. Servants catered to his every whim, singers and dancers entertained him, learned teachers instructed him in the ways of the world. By the time of his marriage at age sixteen to the beautiful princess Yasodhara, he had become a lordly young man, accomplished in all the arts of peace and war. He soon fathered a son.

Yet as the years passed, Siddhattha grew increasingly dissatisfied with his life. He reflected that his current well-being was precarious. It might be snatched from him at any moment by illness or some other mischance. He recognized that, even should he avoid such accidents, his powers and enjoyment would inevitably be eroded by old age, and that, whatever his achievements, death would finally rob him of all that he possessed. True contentment, he concluded, did not lie in worldly success, status, or pleasure. Therefore, in his twenty-ninth year, he abandoned both his family and his previous life in order to search for some surer, more permanent peace.

Initially, he took up the life of a *sammana*, a wandering ascetic. Joining a small community of like-minded seekers, he strove for peace by disciplining and humiliating the body. Spending hours with his limbs painfully contorted, he learned to ignore the discomforts of the body. He went naked, exposed to the elements. His hair grew long and matted and was infested with lice. He became so filthy that, when he moved, it was said, dirt fell from his body in clods. He starved himself nearly to the point of death. Even his fellow sam-manas stood in awe of his exertions. But he did not find that which he sought.

At length he discovered his own way to wisdom, a middle way between the sensual indulgence of his early life and the rigors of asceticism. He meditated deeply, searching within himself, attempting to see through his prejudices and illusions. And so he came to be seated that evening under the Bo tree. There at last, he found what he was looking for. He awoke from the dream-like delusions under which he had lived out his previous life. He became the Buddha, the awakened or enlightened one. He saw all things clearly, just as they are. Shortly thereafter, he began to teach others what he had learned.

So one story goes. Modern scholars have been able to discover little reliable information about the life of the historical founder of Buddhism. He was probably born in the northern portion of the Indian subcontinent, perhaps in what is today the country of Nepal, during the sixth century BCE. Various lines of evidence suggest that he died in 487 BCE.[77] Neither the Buddha nor his immediate disciples wrote down anything about his life or teaching. The oral traditions preserved among his followers were first put in writing more than two centuries after his death. The earliest Buddhist texts were written in Pali, an ancient Indian language. These comprise an extensive body of literature known as the Pali Canon or the Tripitaka, which means "three baskets," signifying the three categories into which these writings were divided: those consisting of rules of the Buddhist monastic orders; sermons or *suttas*; and speculative, philosophical works. All the Buddhist writings quoted in this chapter are taken from the Tripitaka.

We should note that there is also a large body of ancient Buddhist literature that was originally written in Sanskrit, the language of the Upanishads. Thus terms and proper names associated with early Buddhism often appear in English transliteration in different forms, depending on whether they derive from Pali or Sanskrit, for example, "Siddhattha Gotama" (Pali) and "Siddhartha Gautama" (Sanskrit); *nibbana* (Pali) and *nirvana* (Sanskrit); *dhamma* (Pali) and *dharma* (Sanskrit). We will use the transliterations from Pali: thus *nibbana* rather than *nirvana*, except when we want to emphasize concepts in Buddhist thought that derive from the general background of Indian religion. Thus we use *karma* (Sanskrit) rather than *kamma* (Pali).[78]

We should also note that in the course of its historical development, Buddhism divided into a number of different traditions. Perhaps the most significant of these divisions is between the Theravada and Mahayana traditions.[79] We will not discuss the differences between these traditions. Instead we shall focus our discussion on doctrines that are common to all (or nearly all) variants of Buddhism.

In the following section, we shall expound the teachings of Buddha in some detail. For the present, we want to give the reader a brief preview of the issues that will be the focus of our discussion of Buddhism.

---

[77] See T. W. Organ, op. cit., for a good, brief account of our knowledge of the historical Buddha.
[78] See A. K. Warder, *Indian Buddhism*, for a discussion of the linguistic aspects of early Buddhist literature.
[79] See Warder, ibid., for a detailed account of these traditions and other variants of Buddhism.

A great deal of religious thought and literature concerns the possibility of survival or life after death. In the preceding chapter, we saw what the *Upanishads* have to say about what happens to a person after death. Likewise, Christianity and Islam involve very definite views about life after death and about what determines how we shall fare in the hereafter. Although the possibility that we shall continue to exist after our earthly demise carries with it certain risks, for example, being reborn into a miserable future life on earth or being condemned to Hell,[80] it has been generally seen as a source of hope. It holds out the prospect, not merely of continued existence, but of an improved or transformed existence—the hope of a life free from the burdens and limitations of the human condition in this world. Indeed, both critics and proponents of religion often remark that one of the primary functions of religion is precisely to give people such hope.

The Buddha's teachings concerning life after death do not fit into this mold. Those teachings are extremely difficult to understand and difficult for many people to accept. On the one hand, he seems to believe that we do survive the death of the body, but to regard such survival as a curse rather than as a blessing—as a fate worse than death. Indeed, the main point of his doctrine is to teach us how to escape the possibility of life after death. On the other hand, the Buddha sometimes seems to hold that the belief in life after death is a delusion—a fantasy that can never be fulfilled and that serves only to make our lives miserable. The belief in survival is delusional, he explains, because it presupposes that existence of a self or a soul that might continue to exist after the body rots away. But, he says, there is no soul, no self. No soul survives the death of the body, and no self exists in this life.

In what follows we shall try to explain these apparently very different doctrines concerning life after death and to explore the problem of whether they can be made mutually consistent.

---

[80] The atheist philosopher A. J. Ayer, recently deceased, reported having a "near death" experience following a cardiac arrest. Though he thought that the experience was only an illusion, he admitted that it had somewhat shaken his confidence that "My death will be the end of my personal existence." But he added: "I continue to fervently hope that it will be."

THE FOUR NOBLE TRUTHS

What did the Buddha discover under the Bo tree? Although later commentators have produced an enormous body of literature devoted to explaining the Buddha's *dharma* (doctrine or teachings), he himself expressed it very succinctly in four basic principles, which came to be called the Four Noble Truths.

The First Noble Truth is: All existence is *dukkha*. In its ordinary meaning, *dukkha* signifies pain or misery, and it is usually translated as "suffering." In illustrating the First Noble Truth, the Buddha frequently mentions familiar sources of suffering, for example, sickness, old age, death, loss, and despair. However, he believes that dukkha is inherent in all aspects of human existence. In his famous Fire Sermon, he uses the image of burning to suggest the torment of existence:

> All things are on fire. The eye is on fire; forms are on fire; eye-consciousness is on fire; impressions received by the eye are on fire; and whatever sensation, pleasant, unpleasant, or indifferent, originates in dependence on impressions received by the eye, that also is on fire. . . . The ear is on fire; sounds are on fire; . . . the nose is on fire; odors are on fire; . . . the tongue is on fire; tastes are on fire; ideas are on fire; . . . impressions received by the mind are on fire; and whatever originates in dependence on impressions received by the mind, that also is on fire.[81]

This leads us to the Second Noble Truth: The cause of dukkha is *tanha*. *Tanha* literally means "thirst," but is usually translated as "desire" or "craving." According to the Buddha, it is tanha that ignites and continually feeds the fire of dukkha. In the Fire Sermon, he asks, "With what are these (e.g., the eye, ear, mind, etc.) on fire?" And he answers: "With the fire of passion, with the fire of hatred, with the fire of infatuation."[82]

---

[81] H. C. Warren, *Buddhism in Translation*, (New York: Atheneum, 1987), p. 352.
[82] Ibid.

The truth that tanha or desire is the cause of our misery involves two ideas. First, the particular miseries that we experience in our lives result from our failure to fulfill particular desires. We want, for example, comfort, wealth, power, security. To the extent that we fail to attain these things, our frustrated desires torment us. Second and more generally, it is desire that provides the precondition for dukkha. Suffering is possible only for a being who has desires—a being who prefers some circumstances to others, who relishes A and dislikes B, and who loves C and hates D. We suffer when we do not get what we want, or when we get what we do not want. A being without desires, a being utterly indifferent toward all possible outcomes, could not know dukkha.

The truths of dukkha and tanha together sum up the Buddha's diagnosis of the problem of the human condition. The remaining truths spell out his cure for that problem. The Third Noble Truth is: The cure for tanha is *nirodha*. *Nirodha* means "to go out," as a fire goes out. In order to extinguish the fire of dukkha, we must deprive it of its fuel. We must eliminate tanha. We must cease to desire, break our attachments to all the objects of desire, and become utterly indifferent. As the Buddha teaches in the Fire Sermon, once the seeker recognizes the connection between dukkha and tanha elucidated in the Second Noble Truth:

> the learned disciple conceives an aversion for the eye, conceives an aversion for forms, conceives an aversion for eye-consciousness, conceives an aversion for the impressions received by the eye; and whatever sensations . . . originate in dependence on impressions received by the eye, for that he also conceives an aversion. Conceives an aversion for the ear, conceives an aversion for sounds, . . . conceives an aversion for the nose and for odors, . . . conceives an aversion for the tongue and for tastes, . . . conceives an aversion for the body, conceives an aversion for the mind and for ideas . . . and for the impressions received by the mind. . . . And in conceiving this aversion he becomes divested of passion, and by the absence of passion he becomes free.[83]

[83] Ibid., pp. 352–53.

This condition of freedom that the seeker achieves when the fire of dukkha burns out is called *nibbana*. This is the goal toward which all the Buddha's teachings lead.

How are we to achieve this goal? By following the Noble Eightfold Path, the Fourth Noble Truth: The way to achieve nibbana is to follow *magga*. *Magga*, the path, involves right understanding, right thought, right speech, right action, right livelihood, right effort, right mindfulness, and right concentration (i.e., meditation or *samadhi*).[84] We shall not discuss the details of these eight pursuits. At least in early Buddhism, they were thought to require withdrawal from the normal concerns of worldly existence. Those who followed the path had to abandon family life, employment, and political responsibilities. They had to subsist on whatever they received in their begging bowls and turn their full attention toward the search for enlightenment. They became *bhikkus* (monks or nuns), living together with other seekers in a community or *sangha*. The bhikku who successfully pursues the Noble Eightfold Path attained nibbana. (Buddhists differ on the question of whether one can achieve *nibbana* in this life, or whether it comes only after one's death.)

SAMSARA AND ANATTA

The Buddha steadfastly maintained that the Four Noble Truths contain all that we need to know in order to recognize and solve the problem of the human condition. He refused to be drawn into discussions of such metaphysical topics as the creation and fate of the universe, the relation between the soul and the body, and what happens to us after our deaths. Such discussions, he said, profit us nothing and tend to distract us from the goal of nibbana rather than leading us closer to it. "I teach only suffering, the cause of suffering, the extinction of suffering, and the path leading to the extinction of suffering."[85]

---

[84] See W. Rahula, *What the Buddha Taught* (New York: Grove Press, 1959, 1974), chap. 5, for a good discussion of the elements of magga.

[85] See Warren, op. cit., pp. 117–22, for the Buddha's attitude toward "metaphysical" topics.

Nevertheless, the Four Noble Truths raise questions that seem to require some discussion of such metaphysical matters, especially those concerning the nature of the soul or the person. To appreciate these questions and their consequences, let us begin with nirodha, the Third Noble Truth. Why should the cure for dukkha be the elimination of desires rather than the satisfaction of desires? Desires make us suffer only when they go unfulfilled. Why should we not seek to satisfy our desires, rather than get rid of them?

One might reply that we desire more than we need. We never remain satisfied for long with what we have. The scholar, having secured some knowledge, only desires more. The financier, having becomes wealthy, desires even greater wealth, or his desires diversify to include prestige and power. Likewise, it might well be true that we all desire things that, by our very nature, we cannot have, for example, eternal life, omniscience, omnipotence, and perpetual bliss. But even if all this is true, it does not show that we ought to eliminate all our desires. Why should we not simply eliminate those desires that we cannot satisfy and cultivate those desires that we can fulfill? Why must we strive to extinguish all desires?

The first question leads to a second. Suppose we grant that escape from dukkha requires elimination of tanha. Why is that supposed to be so hard? Why do we need to follow magga, the laborious Noble Eightfold Path in order to achieve nibbana, the elimination of desire? Why not take up instead the Noble Sixfold Revolver and use it to blow out the fire of dukkha? How about some pharmacological mind-wipe that would reduce us to unfeeling vegetables? Getting rid of our desires seems like it should be easy. Of course, the methods just suggested for achieving nibbana involve the destruction, physical or psychological, of the person. Those who consider this an objection need to review the First Noble Truth.

Thus the Four Noble Truths present us with two questions. First, why must we eliminate tanha? Second, assuming that we must, why is following the Eightfold Path the best way to achieve this result? To answer these questions, later Buddhists, if not the Buddha himself, felt it necessary to say something about the soul and about what happens to it after the death of the body.

Their answer to our second question can be put in one word, a word already familiar to those who have read our discussion of the Upanishads. That word is *samsara*. As we mentioned previously, Buddhism developed during the same period of intellectual ferment in India that gave rise to the Upanishads, as well as to Jainism and various other religious and philosophical movements.[86] In common with most of these movements, Buddhism adopted the notion of a cycle or wheel of rebirth (*samsara*). My current life is only one among an indefinitely large number of lives that I will live out in the world. When death ends this existence, I will return to the world in a different bodily form and live out another existence, which will end in another death, to be followed by another rebirth, and so on. The conditions in which I find myself in a given life are, in large part, the result of the actions that I performed in my previous lives (*karma*).

It is the doctrine of samsara rather than the Noble Truths *per se* that explains why we must follow magga in order to achieve nibbana. I cannot escape tanha by suicide because suicide does not eliminate my self and my desires. It merely shifts them to another body. Perhaps if I could destroy myself, that would solve all my problems, and something like this self-destruction does seem to be required for achieving nibbana. But self-destruction is hard work. If I die without having eliminated my desires, then these desires will pull me back into the world, into another suffering existence. As in the Upanishads, Buddhism holds that desire, operating through the principle of karma, is the cause of my existence. To seek to eliminate desires by suicidally extinguishing my existence is to get things backward. To extinguish myself, and hence my suffering, I must first eliminate my desires. To finally blow out my desires, to still them forever and so escape the wheel of samsara, requires self-discipline and insight. There is no other way out. The Fourth Noble Truth tells me what I must do in order to eliminate my desires. Only by following the path it lays out can I achieve nibbana.

But what of our first question? The above discussion presupposes that nibbana, the elimination of desire, is the only worthwhile objec-

---

[86] See Organ, op. cit., for a discussion of these movements.

tive. But why should we seek to eliminate desires rather than to satisfy them (or to eliminate all desires rather than eliminate some and fulfill others)? The addition of the doctrine of samsara to the Four Noble Truths makes the Third Noble Truth, nirodha, look even harder to justify. Clearly in any one life, there will be many desires that I do not have the power to fulfill. But given dozens, or hundreds, or thousands, or millions of lives to work with, it seems that nothing should be beyond my power. Indeed, the Upanishads teach that I can satisfy even the desire to become God. By concentrating all my efforts on satisfying this desire and disciplining myself to ignore every lesser objective, I can liberate my atman, the ultimate being within me, from all the limitations of the human condition. I can achieve moksha, oneness with Brahman.

Up to this point our exposition of the Buddha's dharma has made it seem not very different from the views propounded in the *Upanishads*. Both regard ordinary human existence as a deeply unsatisfying condition. Both identify desire or attachment as the source of this condition and both propose that we can free ourselves from our unsatisfactory existence by eliminating (at least some) desires. What then distinguishes the Buddhist view from the teachings of the Upanishads? Is *nibbana* just the Pali word for *moksha*?

The Buddhist explanation of why we have to eliminate all of our desires in order to escape from dukkha is what distinguishes Buddhism from the Upanishadic system. The Upanishads teach that we must extinguish all our lesser desires in order to satisfy our greatest desire, namely, the desire to be God, the desire for a perfect, secure, eternal existence. Buddhism holds that it is this desire more than any other that we must extinguish in ourselves. Indeed, this desire for the unlimited enhancement and perfection of our own existence is the desire from which all our lesser desires ultimately derive. Desires for sensual pleasures, wealth, power, and so forth, all aim in their various ways at promoting the well-being of the self. We find that the satisfaction of these lesser desires fails to satisfy us because, even when we achieve pleasure, wealth, and power, we remain subject to the basic limitations of the human condition, to sickness, old age, death, the wheel of rebirth. We recognize that perfect well-being requires liberation from all these limitations. The desire for the well-being of the self is constant, all that changes is our knowledge of what is required to achieve such well-being.

But why must we extinguish this desire? If the desire for the well-being of the self is the very spark of our existence, why should we try to blow it out, rather than to satisfy it? The desire for personal perfection is indeed the spark of our existence and, if it were satisfiable, then the solution to the misery of human existence might lie, as the Upanishads say it does, in the pursuit of a God-like, perfect existence. But this desire cannot be satisfied. It cannot be satisfied because the very thing whose well-being it seeks and whose existence it aims to perfect, the self, does not exist.

The doctrine of *anatta* (Sanskrit, *anatman*), the doctrine that there is no self or soul, is the most distinctive feature of Buddhist thought. Walpola Rahula, a distinguished modern expositor of Buddhism, writes,

> Buddhism stands unique in the history of human thought in denying the existence of a Soul, Self, or Atman. According to the teaching of the Buddha, the idea of self is an imaginary, false belief which has no corresponding reality, and it produces harmful thoughts of "me" and "mine," selfish desire, craving, attachment . . . pride, egoism, and other defilements, impurities, and problems. . . . To this false view can be traced all the evil in the world.[87]

Anatta is also perhaps the most difficult concept in Buddhism to explain satisfactorily. We shall explore these difficulties momentarily. But before turning to them, let us emphasize how the doctrine of anatta supports the Third Noble Truth. We have asked why we should seek relief from dukkha by extinguishing all our desires rather than by satisfying (all or some) of them. The answer is now clear. All our desires concern the enhancement of the self; all aim at making the self better off in some way. Since there is no self, none of these desires can be satisfied. Since we know that unsatisfied desire is the source of our suffering, it is apparent that dukkha will cease only if we give up all our desires. Therefore, the only cure for dukkha is nirodha.

[87] Rahula, p. 51.

So this is how anatta explains the Third Noble Truth. But how are we to explain anatta? According to Buddhism, what we call, speaking in purely conventional terms, the "self" consists in a collection of five "heaps" or "aggregates," the five *khandas*. The first khanda is the body, *rupakkhanda*, sometimes translated as "form"; the second, *vedanakkhanda*, consists of sensations or sense impressions, for example, sensations of color, odor, taste, and so forth; the third, *sannakkhanda*, often translated as "perceptions," is probably best thought of as representing the judgments we make on the basis of sensation, for example, the judgment that this rose is red, or that this fish stinks; the fourth, *samkharakkhanda*, translated as "mental formations" or "dispositions," includes all the various types of mental activities in which we engage, for example, desire, will, emotion, attention, and so forth; the fifth aggregate, *vinnanakkhanda*, usually translated as "consciousness," represents our awareness of our bodies, sensations, perceptions, mental formations as our own (it represents our sense of being the subject of our experiences and the agent of our actions). Each of these five is itself a collection ("heap") of distinct elements; for example, our body consists of various distinct parts, we have many different types of sensations, and so forth.

In ordinary life we think of particular collections of the five khandas as distinct individuals, and we give them names such as "Siddhattha," "Nagasena," "George," "Arlene," and so forth. Further, the particular collections of khandas that constitute a given individual are related to each other. For example, Arlene's bodily sense organs determine which sensations she will have, which in turn determine her judgments or perceptions, which determine her mental activities, which are the objects of her sense of self-consciousness.

This picture resembles, in some respects, the Upanishadic picture of the *jiva* or individual self that consists of the *koshas*, the five sheaths. But there is one big difference between the two pictures. In the Upanishads, when the koshas are peeled back, what is found inside is the *atman*, the true, eternal, unlimited self. The self is like the pith tightly wrapped in the leaves of a reed. For Buddhism however, the individual person is like an onion. When you peel back the layers, what you find inside is . . . nothing. The khandas do not contain a real self or soul. Our true selves are not something bound within the khandas. Rather, the individual person simply is a particular collection of the five khandas, nothing more.

The khandas do not contain a self or a soul. Neither does any one or several of the khandas constitute a self or a soul. Neither the body, nor the sensations, nor the consciousness associated with a particular individual, represents that individual's self or soul. Thus, no soul is found either within the khandas or among them. Buddhism teaches,

> As respects all form (body), past, future, or present . . . the correct view in light of the highest knowledge is as follows, "This is not mine; this is not I: this is not my ego." As respects all sensation, . . . as respects all perception, . . . as respects all predispositions, . . . as respects all consciousness . . . the correct view in light of the highest knowledge is as follows: "This is not mine; this is not I; this is not my ego."[88]

Although there is no self, the illusion or delusion of self does exist. We think of ourselves not as a mere collection of khandas, but as a real persisting being. Consequently, we desire to promote the welfare of, to ensure the continued existence of, and to enhance the perfection of, that being. Since these desires falsely presuppose the existence of the self, they can never be satisfied. Lacking satisfaction, they lead only to suffering. To end this suffering, we must give up these desires. In order to give them up, we need to recognize the falsity of the belief in self on which they depend. The recognition of anatta leads to, and is required for, nibbana:

> Perceiving [that there is no self] the learned disciple conceives an aversion for form, conceives an aversion for sensation, conceives an aversion for perception, conceives an aversion for predispositions, conceives an aversion for consciousness. And in conceiving this aversion he becomes divested of passion, and by the absence of passion he becomes free; . . . and he knows that rebirth is exhausted, . . . and that he is no more for this world.[89]

[88] Warren, p. 147.
[89] Ibid.

CAN BUDDHISM TEACH BOTH
ANATTA AND SAMSARA?

We have now both explained why we must extinguish tanha in order to escape dukkha (the Third Noble Truth, nirodha) and why we must follow the Noble Eightfold Path in order to extinguish tanha (the Fourth Noble Truth, magga). Unfortunately, our answers seem to be inconsistent. We have justified nirodha by saying that, since there is no self, our desires for self-gratification cannot be satisfied and so we must give them up. We have argued that suicide will not extinguish tanha because suicide fails to destroy the self, and merely results in the self's transfer, complete with its desires, to a new body. Thus we have invoked the doctrine of anatta in defense of nirodha, and invoked the doctrine of samsara in defense of magga. However, the latter doctrine apparently asserts exactly what the former denies, namely, that the self exists and that the same self persists through different lives. No wonder the Buddha didn't want to talk about the soul and what happens to it after death.

The easy way out of this problem would be to give up either anatta or samsara. But, as we have seen, each doctrine plays a crucial role in justifying the Four Noble Truths. Furthermore, while Buddhists have disagreed among themselves during the centuries since the Buddha's death on many matters concerning their dharma, nearly all have agreed in accepting both anatta and samsara.[90] So we need to look for a way to make these doctrines mutually consistent.

One way in which Buddhist thinkers have sought to reconcile samsara and anatta is by arguing that samsara need not involve the existence of a persistent self that is present in different bodies and lives out different lives. They use the image of a flame being passed from one candle to another. Though we speak of the flame being "passed" from candle A to candle B, A's flame and B's flame are physically distinct things. No physical thing has been transferred from A to B. What has happened, rather, is that the burning wick of

---

[90] Rahula, pp. 55–66.

candle A has caused candle B to ignite. Just so, when we say that a person is reborn, there has been no transfer of a self or soul from one body to another. Rather, the life of one person, say Richard, has caused and shaped the life of another, Arlene, in such a way that we can consider Arlene's life a continuation (in some sense) of Richard's life. It is not that Arlene is Richard, but that her life is as it is, because his life was as it was.

On this view, what we think of as "Richard" is just a collection of khandas. On Richard's death, this particular group of khandas will cease to exist. His body will rot away; his sensations, which depend on his body, will cease; and likewise his perceptions, his mental activities, and his consciousness will cease. But it is possible that, because these "Richard khandas" existed and were as they were, another group of khandas, having certain characteristics, will come into existence. This group of khandas will constitute a new individual, Arlene. Nothing that was part of Richard continues to exist in Arlene. Nevertheless, it might be true, for example, that because Richard had various desires, Arlene will have similar desires, or that Richard's having certain sorts of knowledge will cause Arlene to have the same sorts of knowledge. In this way, Richard's craving and the misery it produced in him can be, as it were, passed on to Arlene, even though Arlene and Richard are distinct persons and have no parts in common. Arlene exists and suffers because of Richard's existence and suffering.

On the other hand, were Richard to extinguish his desires, then when he dies, no new individual, no further collection of khandas, would be produced as a result of his life. He would not only extinguish his own suffering, but also prevent any further suffering from arising because of his desire.

On this picture, samsara involves no eternally existing souls passing from body to body, but a chain or series of distinct individuals, each of whose lives is shaped by the lives of the earlier members of the series. If the latest individual in the series achieves nibbana, then the series comes to an end. If not, then the series will continue according to the laws of karma—the desires of earlier members being "continued" in the desires of latter members of the series, a chain of suffering.

Although this picture of samsara is certainly possible, it raises certain problems. It would be nice of Richard to submit to the discipline of the Noble Eightfold Path in order to extinguish his desires and, thereby ending, not only his own suffering, but also preventing Arlene from suffering. However, Richard can get rid of his own desires and his own suffering simply by ending his own life, by whatever method. In pursuing nibbana by following the Noble Eightfold Path, rather than by some quick and dirty means, Richard is doing a favor for Arlene (i.e., he is making sure that she won't exist, and hence, won't suffer). But he is doing this at some expense to himself. He could end his own miserable existence much more quickly and with much less trouble. So unless Richard is a very compassionate person, a person motivated by something other than a desire for individual nibbana, he might take the easy way out. That would be bad for other people, for all those who will exist and suffer because he failed to properly extinguish his desires. But it wouldn't do Richard any harm.

Perhaps, then, it would be better to think of samsara as involving the rebirth of the same person or self. Otherwise, nibbana will be cheap—everybody will achieve it, at least for themselves, whenever they die, regardless of how they lived. In that case, only the most altruistic of us will be motivated to follow the Noble Eightfold Path.

But if we say that the self persists through rebirth, are we not giving up the doctrine of anatta? Buddhists have interpreted anatta in a variety of different ways.[91] This is understandable because the doctrine bristles with difficulties. Rahula, for example, writes that, "The idea of self is an imaginary, false belief" that "produces harmful thoughts of 'me' and 'mine,' selfish desire, . . . pride, egoism."[92] But, if there is no self, who has this imaginary belief, who thinks these harmful thoughts of "me" and "mine?" Belief, thoughts, desires, feelings of pride, and dispositions toward egotism are not the sorts of things that can exist on their own. There must be somebody who has these beliefs, thinks these thoughts, feels these feelings. So, at any

---

[91] See A. K. Warder, *Indian Buddhism*, 2d ed. (Delhi: Motilal Banardisass Indological Publisher, 1980), chap. 9, for a discussion of the different interpretations of this doctrine in the early history of Buddhism.
[92] Rahula, op. cit., p. 51.

rate, many people would argue. This makes it tempting to suppose that the doctrine of anatta is not intended to contradict our conventional beliefs about selves, for example, not to contradict my belief that I am the same self at different points in my life-history. Perhaps the doctrine should not even be so interpreted as to exclude the possibility that the same self could exist in other bodies and live different lives.

What is crucial about the doctrine of anatta, at least in relation to the Four Noble Truths, is not so much that it denies the existence of the self, but that it denies the perfectability of the self. Both the Upanishads and Buddhism agree that the well-spring of all human desire is the craving for a perfect, unlimited, God-like existence. Only that would ultimately satisfy us. We will remain bound to the wheel of samsara, caught up in dukkha, until this desire is either satisfied or extinguished. Buddhism counsels us to seek to extinguish this desire. In order to justify this advice, it is not necessary to argue that there is no self. It is necessary to argue only that the self can never escape the limitations that constitute the human condition—the limitations that Buddhism calls the khandas. The self may exist in different bodies, but never exist except in some material body. The self might experience many different sensations, but can never know the world except through the sensations determined by a body's sense organs. Try as it might, the self can never put aside the imperfections of human thought, human feeling, and human consciousness. So long as the self exists at all, it can only exist within some particular collection of the five khandas.

Although the self can never transcend its limitations, it constantly seeks to do so. Thinking, falsely, that such perfection is possible, the self desires it. This never-to-be-satisfied desire makes a hell of this life and impels the self to grasp at further life and endure further misery in rebirth. The enlightened self, realizing that it can never obtain the only thing that it most desires, will seek to extinguish this desire and, thereby, terminate its fruitless and miserable quest for perfection.

If the above discussion is on the right track, Buddhists need deny only the existence of atman, the perfect, unlimited self of the Upanishads, in order to justify the Third Noble Truth. They can admit that there is a self that persists through different bodies and different lives, while still maintaining that the cure for dukkha lies in the extinction of desire rather than in its satisfaction. Of course, Buddhist thinkers have been concerned with more than just attempting to defend the Four Noble Truths and there might be reasons for denying the reality of any self at all, rather than merely denying the perfect atman. Certainly many Buddhist thinkers do want to deny that there is any self, even in the most conventional sense of the term. In that case it will be necessary either to reject the doctrine of samsara or to search further for an interpretation of it that is compatible with anatta.

CONCLUSION

It has not been our purpose here to pronounce the final word on anatta and samsara. Rather, we have sought to show how these doctrines fit into the overall structure of the Buddhist picture of reality. We have sought to show what problems they solve and what problems they create for that view. Perhaps, ultimately, there is no way of reconciling them. Be that as it may, the project of reconciling anatta and samsara has been one of the central intellectual problems in Buddhist thought. The authors' desires will be more than satisfied if our readers have gained from our discussion a sense of the nature and extent of that problem.

7

Does Public Morality Depend on Religion?

▼ ▼ ▼

Confucius on Politics and Religion

In this chapter we examine the role of religion in maintaining public order or morality. Many people suppose that religious belief provides an indispensable prop for civil order. The arm of the law might be long, but its reach is limited. Fear of human law enforcement can never suffice for keeping everyone on the straight and narrow path of morality. No society can afford a big enough police force to keep everybody constantly under surveillance. Only if citizens believe that their every action is observed by a superhuman judge, who has unlimited power to punish their transgressions and reward their good behavior, will they be truly convinced that crime never pays. It therefore behooves a society to do what it can to foster such beliefs.

This sounds like a cheap and efficient strategy for promoting law and order, but some thinkers find it deeply repulsive. They argue that it undermines human dignity and replaces genuine moral feelings with slavish fear and groveling. They further claim that it is entirely unnecessary. Appeals to reason, backed by customary methods of law enforcement, are adequate for maintaining public order. Religious belief, or lack of it, should be a private matter and not a concern of state policy.

Both positions have some appeal, and the question, of whether belief in divinely administered rewards and punishments is necessary for preserving public order, continues to be actively debated. In our exploration of this question, however, we turn to the thought of ancient China. Confucius, his followers, and his opponents devoted considerable attention to the problem of how social harmony ought to be maintained. Their debates contain perhaps the earliest well-reasoned discussion of the role that belief in supernatural rewards and punishments might play in solving this problem. They also raise the further question of whether the most important contribution of religion to morality has anything to do with rewards and punishments.

VOLTAIRE'S ADMIRATION OF CONFUCIAN VIEWS

Confucius was the first East Asian philosopher to acquire a substantial reputation in Europe. Jesuit missionaries returning from China first brought his work to the attention of European intellectuals in the seventeenth century CE. Over the next hundred years, his philosophy became well-known and often won enthusiastic praise. The French philosopher Voltaire became a devoted admirer, writing that in his extensive study of Confucius's works: "I have never found in them anything but the purest morality, without the slightest tinge of charlatanism."[93] What attracted Voltaire, a skeptical, secularist, progressive thinker to the teachings of a Chinese sage who died more than two millennia before Voltaire's birth?

Voltaire was part of an intellectual movement now called the Enlightenment that spread across Europe in the late seventeenth and early eighteenth centuries. The Enlightenment philosophers severely criticized traditional European thinking and institutions. They focused their criticisms particularly on religious dogmatism, as well as on the public power and influence of the church. Their opponents argued that the attacks of Enlightenment skepticism on established

---

[93] Quoted in H. G. Creel, *Confucius and the Chinese Way* (New York: Harper and Row, 1949), p. 261, from Voltaire's *Philosophical Dictionary*.

religion were not only an offense against God, but also an assault on the foundations of social order.

According to the traditional European theory, the authority both of the King and of the aristocracy, their right to command the obedience of the people, came from God. Thus, an attack on religious belief was an attack on the existing political hierarchy. Furthermore, it was thought that threats of divine punishment and promises of heavenly reward were required in order to maintain public morality. Should people ever decide that they need not fear Hell and could not hope for Heaven, their behavior would become uncontrollable. Society would dissolve into a mass of competing individuals, each seeking nothing but his or her own advantage, each restrained only by the weak and fallible efforts of human law enforcement. Society, the traditionalists argued, must promote religious belief if we are to enjoy peace and public order.

But the Enlightenment philosophers maintained that public morality and social order need not rest on religion. They argued that human reason, unencumbered by religious dogma, could provide the basis of a well-ordered society. It was here that these philosophers thought they had found an ally in Confucius. As they interpreted his views, he had taught a system of morality that made no appeal to supernatural sanctions. Confucius held that people could be taught to live together in harmony without threatening them with divine punishment or promising them a heavenly reward. Furthermore, this was not just an idealistic theory. Confucian philosophy had provided the intellectual foundation of political authority and public morality in China for nearly two thousand years. The relative stability and prosperity of the Chinese empire (which, perhaps, seemed more impressive seen from distant Europe than up close) were taken to show that a social order based solely on human reason represented a practical possibility.[94]

The eighteenth-century debate about the role of religion in maintaining social order continues down to the present. In contemporary America, many people argue that religion should be kept out of

[94] See Creel, ibid., pp. 254–78, for a more extensive discussion of the Enlightenment view of Confucianism.

politics—that the government has no business promoting religious belief and that we ought to maintain a "wall of separation" between church and state. Others believe that we have gone too far in creating a secular society—that, in excluding religious observance from our schools and other public institutions, we are undermining the standards of moral behavior necessary for successful social life.

Where does Confucius really stand on these issues? Was he, indeed, a proponent of a purely secular morality? Did he see any role for religion in the creation or preservation of social order? To investigate his views on these topics, it is helpful to look, not only at his own work, but at the work of other ancient Chinese philosophers. It was in ancient China where questions concerning the role of religion in politics received their first serious philosophical discussion. As we shall discover, the Confucian account of the place of religion in a well-ordered society is more complicated than the philosophers of the European Enlightenment realized.

LIFE AND TIMES OF CONFUCIUS

Though there is an old and extensive literature on Confucius in Chinese, the facts of his personal life are difficult to establish.[95] Probably he was born around 550 BCE and died around 480. His family belonged to the aristocracy of the northern Chinese state of Lu, but at the time of his birth the family was neither wealthy nor powerful. His family name was Kong. "Confucius" is a Latinized pronunciation of the title later given him by his disciples, "Kongzi," which means "Master Kong." Like other members of his class, Confucius's early ambition was to secure an official position in the administration of the state.

In Confucius's time, China was divided up into a large number of states, each having its own ruling family and its own aristocracy, that is, those families entitled by tradition to participate in governing the

---

[95] Our account of Confucius's life is based on Creel, ibid. He discusses the conflicting accounts of Confucius's life in the Chinese sources (pp. 7–11).

state. Nominally, all the states recognized the authority of a single imperial dynasty, the Zhou. But the Zhou emperors were without real power and all the states conducted their own affairs. The states warred incessantly against each other and taxed their populations heavily in order to pay for this warfare. Taxes also went to support the ruler's court and bureaucracy. Internal strife and official corruption were constant sources of complaint. Rulers often feared their own officials and subjects more than their external enemies. It was common both for aristocratic officials and for nonaristocratic subjects (merchants, artisans, and farmers) to leave their native states either in search of better opportunities elsewhere or to escape oppressive conditions at home.

Confucius shared with a great many of his contemporaries a deep dissatisfaction at the general lack of peace and good government that prevailed in China. Originally, he had hoped to take a direct role in reforming these conditions by rising to a position of political influence, but he was unable to secure any such position, either in Lu or in any of the many other states that he visited. So instead he devoted himself to scholarly pursuits. He studied the historical records of the Zhou dynasty. He learned poetry and music. He became an expert in *li*, that is, in the proper conduct of rituals and public ceremonies. Eventually, he acquired a considerable reputation both for his learning and for his character. A group of followers were drawn to him and he began to see himself primarily as a teacher.

Our most important record of Confucius's teachings is a collection called the *Analects* (*Lunya*). The *Analects* consist of (generally very brief) accounts of what Confucius said or did on particular occasions. They are not systematically organized and might contain material written long after Confucius's death. Nevertheless, they provide the best access we have to his philosophy.

Ironically in becoming a teacher, Confucius gained the sort of influence on public affairs that he had vainly sought in his quest for public office. During his own lifetime several of his students rose to positions of power, and after his death, they continued to spread his teachings and to further develop his ideas. In time, a Confucian "school" or tradition of philosophy was created, and ultimately Confucianism became, as it were, the official philosophy of government in China.[96] Through China's influence and example, Confucius's teachings also served as the foundation of political philosophy in Korea, Japan, and Vietnam.

Confucius on Political Authority

The following story in the *Analects* neatly sums up Confucius's account of the basis of political authority. A student asks Confucius what is most important for governing a society. The master replies that the ruler needs weapons to defend the society, stores of food both to feed his officials and also to distribute to the people in times of hardship, and the confidence of the people. The student then asks, if the ruler must do without one of these, which should he forego? "Weapons," Confucius replies. The student persists: if the ruler must sacrifice one of the remaining two, which should it be? The master said, "Food. For all down through history, death has come to all men, and yet society survives; but the people who have no confidence in their rulers are undone" (12.7).[97]

According to Confucius, the ruler's ability to govern effectively, that is, the ruler's political authority, and a society's ability to preserve itself as a functioning community, depend on the people's trust or confidence in the ruler. Living in sixth-century China, Confucius's account naturally presupposes that political authority will reside in a single ruler, who may delegate part of his authority to the officials who administer his realm. However, as a practical matter, authority is hierarchically distributed in nearly every form of human political society. That is, there will be a relatively small number of people who make the decisions and who ensure that the rest of us abide by them.

---

[96] See H. G. Creel, *Chinese Thought* (Chicago: University of Chicago Press, 1953), for an account of the later development of Confucianism.

[97] All references to the *Analects* in the text are to the translation by E. R. Hughes in *Chinese Philosophy in Classical Times* (London: Dent, 1982) unless otherwise indicated. The *Analects* are organized into twenty books (chapters) and each passage in numbered within each book. We will give the book and passage number in parentheses in the text, e.g., 12.7. This passage occurs on p. 23 of Hughes's translation.

In democratic societies, the decision makers are elected to their positions, but between elections, the rest of us have to do what they say. (If you have any doubts about this, try not paying your federal income taxes for a few years.) So Confucius's point can be put in general terms: however a society's decision makers get their positions of authority, their ability to govern effectively depends on the confidence of the people.

How does the ruler gain the people's confidence? Here success depends, Confucius says, on the ruler's own moral character. "If the ruler is right in himself, things will get done without his giving orders. When he is not right in himself, he may give orders, but they will not be obeyed" (13.6).[98] He believes that the ruler's own moral power or moral example exerts a natural influence on the ruler's subjects, drawing them in and making them willing to obey.

> If those in the higher ranks of society be devoted to ritual, then none of the common people can dare not to venerate them. If they be lovers of justice, then none of the common people can dare not to obey them. If they be worthy of confidence, then none of the common people can dare to prevaricate. If that be the state of affairs (in a country), then the common people will come to it from all parts, carrying their babies on their backs. (13.4)[99]

In winning the people's confidence, there is no substitute for being worthy of that confidence. It cannot be gained by pandering to popular opinion. "Men of true breeding are in harmony with the people, [even when] they do not agree with them; but men of no breeding agree with the people, and yet are not in harmony with them" (13.23).[100] Nor can the people's confidence be gained by coercion or force.

> If you try to lead people . . . by means of punishments, they will try to avoid them without any conscience whatever. If, however, you try to lead them by your own moral power, and order their lives by means of rituals, their consciences will act and they will flock around you. (2.3)[101]

---

[98] Ibid., p. 25.
[99] Ibid.
[100] Ibid., p. 22.
[101] Ibid., p. 26.

According to Confucius, rule by threat of force is counterproductive. Rather than inspiring confidence, it leads people to seek to evade the ruler's commands, and it fosters deceit in them. Since they feel no confidence in the ruler, they have no compunction about disobeying whenever they think they can get away with it.

If authority depends on moral character, in what does good moral character consist? Confucius mentions many different components of good character, such as courage, loyalty, honesty, and several others. But there is one character trait, a master virtue, which sums them up, namely, *ren*. *Ren* has no convenient equivalent in English. Some translators render it as "human-heartedness." But the idea behind ren can be captured in a familiar sounding idiom: "What you do not wish done to yourself, do not do to others" (75.23).[102] This is sometimes called the negative version of the Golden Rule, "Do unto others as you would have them do unto you."

Ren is a matter of being able to see things from the other person's point of view, of being willing to take the other person's feelings and interests into account in your decision making. It is a matter of asking yourself, "How would I feel if someone did that to me?" The ruler who has *ren*, makes his decisions in accordance with these considerations.

> A human-hearted ruler wants security for himself, and so he makes others secure. He wishes to get a wider sphere of influence, so he extends other people's spheres of influence. (6.28)[103]

When a ruler asked about how to govern in accordance with ren, Confucius replies:

> In public behave as you would in the presence of an honored guest. Set the people their public tasks as if you were conducting a great sacrifice. The treatment you would not have for yourself, do not hand out to other people. Then there will be no resentment against you. (12.2)[104]

[102] Ibid., p. 30.
[103] Ibid., p. 19.
[104] Ibid.

How is ren acquired and made effective? Confucius makes two observations here. First, he says that the acquisition of ren begins in the most basic aspects of your personal life, that is, in your relation to your family. "Being a good son," he says, "is the root of a man's character" (1.2).[105] His idea is that the family is a microcosm of the human community. You learn to be a good subject by first learning to be a good son or a good daughter. You master the qualities required for good relations with your neighbors by first learning what it takes to be a good brother or a good sister. In becoming a good parent, you acquire the traits of character that will make you a good ruler. Ren starts small. It begins in your relations with those closest to you. It expands outward. As you deal with an even larger circle of people, you transfer the attitudes cultivated within the family to your role in the larger society. When Confucius was asked why he was not taking part in the administration of his country, he replied, "*The Book of Documents* says, 'Be filial, only be filial and friendly with your brothers, and you will be helping in the administration of the country' " (2.21).[106]

The idea that family relations are the basis of moral character is familiar in our own culture. But Confucius's second observation about ren needs more explanation. The passages we have quoted from the *Analects* frequently mention rituals, ceremonies, and sacrifices. These are referred to collectively by Confucius as *li*. The term *li* originally referred to the public sacrifices and ceremonies that the ancient Chinese employed to win the favor of heaven and in honoring the ancestors of the ruling families. These were great public occasions in which gorgeously costumed celebrants carried out elaborate rituals to the accompaniment of music. Confucius, also used *li* to refer to the many small "ceremonies" or "rituals" that are performed in our public lives. Every culture has its own forms of good manners or politeness, such as proper greetings, formulaic ways of expressing gratitude or deference, ways of showing respect, as well as its solemn ceremonies. Think of how we inaugurate our presidents, celebrate marriages, and conduct trials, funerals, or religious services. Consider how we

---

[105] *Confucius: The Analects*, trans. D. C. Lau (New York: Penguin Books, 1979), p. 59.
[106] Hughes, op. cit., p. 13.

address our parents, bid farewell to our friends, and conduct ourselves when we are introduced to strangers. All of these sorts of rituals, large and small, are part of what Confucius means by *li*.

But what is the relevance of li to ren? Confucius says that our willingness to take other people's interests into account is the "raw material" of ren, but that li is "the means for putting it into effect" (15.17). Even if my heart is in the right place, it would be very difficult for me to treat other people properly, if I always have to decide how to act on a case-by-case basis. Li provides me with a repertoire of almost automatic behaviors by which I might show my consideration for others and that others will instantly recognize as expressions of such consideration. Having such a set of responses might be less necessary for dealing with good friends, but it is invaluable for guiding my conduct toward casual acquaintances or strangers. A similar sentiment was expressed in the advice attributed to William Paley, "Manners are minor morals."

Li also tells me how to behave on those great occasions, which seldom come up in the course of day-to-day life, and on which I might be too overcome by the occasion to deliberately think through what I ought to do. Li gives me a way to express emotions, such as the honor I feel on being presented to the president, the grief I experience at the death of my parent or my child, the sympathy I feel for another's calamity, or the awe I sense on entering the house of God. Li gives me ways of expressing myself and communicating my intentions to others that I do not have to make up as I go along. Li, without the good intentions, the "raw material" behind it, is empty. But, without li, the good intentions can be difficult to express in my conduct or to recognize in the conduct of others.

Beyond giving me the means to express ren, li also has an important political function. Confucius says, "the making of a state depends on our capacity for mutual yielding which is embodied in the traditional rituals" (4.13).[107] A society's public ceremonies help to impress both on those who conduct them and on those who witness them a sense of being involved in something larger than themselves. Confucius

[107] Ibid., p. 25.

always emphasizes that a human society is not just the collection of individuals who currently inhabit a territory. Its institutions were founded by people who lived long ago. It would not exist today if not for the efforts of the ancestors of its current citizens. Likewise, society extends into the future. Our actions today will shape the lives of people who do not yet exist. We inherit a community from our ancestors and pass it down to our descendents. It is not only fitting, it is essential for the survival of a society, that its members have a sense of gratitude for those who went before and a sense of responsibility to those who will come after: that they should feel awe at being a part of this continuing community. "To sacrifice to the spirits of one's ancestors," Confucius observes, "is like being in the company of the spirits"(3.12).[108]

But why should we not just tell people about their place in their community? Why not just explain to them what they owe to their ancestors and their descendants? Because, Confucius says, such public ceremonies move us in ways and impress us with things that we cannot fully explain or put into words.

> Someone asked to have the Great Sacrifice (in the Royal Ancestral Temple) explained, and the Master said, "I do not know. The man who could explain that would have everything in this world of ours as plainly revealed as this;" and he pointed to the palm of his hand. (3.11)[109]

But one need not be able to explain the Great Sacrifice in order to be impressed by it and drawn into it.

So the moral power on which the ruler's authority depends consists in the expression of the ruler's ren, which will be made effective through li. Does this mean that if you cultivate your ren and embody it in li, then you will rise to a position of power and influence? No. Confucius never says that having moral power and influence guarantees political success. Nor should ren be pursued simply as a means to achieve power, or ever abandoned in order to obtain power.

---

[108] Ibid., p. 26.
[109] Ibid.

Wealth and high station, these are what men would like to have; but if they cannot be obtained in conformity with principle they must not be held. Poverty and low station, these are what men dislike but if they cannot be avoided without controvertion of principle, they must be accepted. (4.5)[110]

For Confucius, the relationship between having moral power and achieving political power is problematic. He thinks that the ruler cannot govern successfully without possessing the moral power required to earn the people's confidence. But governing successfully is not just a matter of attaining or holding onto power over the people. A ruler who lacks moral power might be able to maintain political power through force and cunning. Such a ruler will always be insecure, constantly threatened by plots, rebellion, and desertion. But Confucius had too much experience with the world to deny that such rulers will sometimes be able to hold onto their power. Confucius once commented: "For a man to live he must be upright," but then he added, "If he is not upright and keeps alive, it is a stroke of luck [for him]" (6.17).[111] Notice that, while Confucius believes that the wicked are likely to perish, he does not deny that they may occasionally get lucky.

The uncertainty of human affairs is such that no amount of virtue can guarantee success. For that reason, Confucius feels, we should concentrate not on achieving power, but on being worthy of it. The most important question is not whether we succeed, but how we do it. Advising his students on the pursuit of power, Confucius concluded:

If the Way prevails [i.e., if things are as they ought to be] among the states, make yourselves prominent. If it does not prevail, then keep in retirement. If it prevails in your area, it is a disgrace to be poor and humble. If it does not prevail, it is a disgrace to be rich and honored. (8.13)[112]

---

[110] Ibid., p. 20.
[111] Ibid., p. 14.
[112] Ibid., p. 21.

CONFUCIUS'S CRITICS

Though Confucianism eventually emerged as the dominant philosophy of government in China, it did not lack for critics. Especially during the two centuries following Confucius's death, his followers engaged in heated debates with other Chinese philosophers over the merits of his views.[113] Much of the debate focused on his claims about the influence of the ruler's moral power.

Confucius says that the ruler's moral power will inspire confidence in the people, which will lead naturally to their obeying the ruler's commands. His critics replied that human beings by their very nature are motivated only to seek their own advantage. People have likes and dislikes. They strive to get what they like and avoid what they dislike. That is the whole story about human motivation. Inevitably the ruler must sometimes ask his subjects to do things they do not like to do (e.g., paying taxes) and to refrain from doing things they enjoy (e.g., smoking opium). In such cases no amount of moral power will secure their obedience.

What did Confucius's critics offer as an alternative? Their motto was, "A ruler can get more with moral power and a sword, than he can with just moral power." That is, they believed that the ruler could secure the obedience of the people only by employing rewards and punishments. The wise ruler uses human nature rather than struggling to change it. People will do whatever they perceive to be to their advantage. To get them to do what he wants them to do, the ruler need only convince them that it is to their advantage to do so. Suppose the ruler wants people to pay taxes. Naturally people would prefer to keep all their income for their own use. The ruler announces that all those who fail to pay taxes will be cut in half with a bamboo saw. (A favorite Chinese method of revenue enhancement.) People will certainly prefer giving up half their incomes to being sawn in half, so pure self-interest will lead them to comply with the ruler's direc-

---

[113] These debates are explored in detail in A. C. Graham, *Disputers of the Tao* (LaSalle, Ill.: Open Court, 1989) and B. I. Schwartz, *The World of Thought in Ancient China* (Cambridge, Mass.: Harvard University Press, 1985).

tives. The ruler might use rewards to change peoples preferences in a similar manner, for example, by offering large incomes to those willing to run the risks of military service. Han Fei (d. 233 BCE), one of Confucius's most notable critics, summed up this approach very neatly:

> The empire can be ruled only by utilizing human nature. Men have likes and dislikes; thus they can be controlled by means of rewards and punishments. On this basis prohibitions and commands can be put in operation and a complete system of government set up. The ruler need only hold these two handles [reward and punishment] firmly, in order to maintain his supremacy.[114]

The wise ruler uses the "two handles" to steer the people in the direction he wants them to go. Should the ruler fail to grasp the handles, people will move in whatever direction their search for personal advantage leads them, regardless of the ruler's moral power

MOZI'S UTOPIA OF ALL-EMBRACING LOVE

Some of those who rejected Confucius's views on the political significance of moral power held morality in contempt and were interested only in mastering the techniques of political power, but others claimed to be animated by the highest moral ideals. This was true of a school of philosophers who took their inspiration from a (perhaps mythical) figure named Mozi, or Master Mo.

Mozi was alleged to have lived during the century following Confucius's death. Even more than Confucius, he was scathingly critical of the aristocratic system of government, and he is supposed to have organized a secret society dedicated to changing it. His thoughts were written down in a book called after himself, the Mozi.[115] Mozi's dominant idea was that human society should operate according to

[114] Creel (1953), op. cit., p. 149.
[115] See Graham (1989), op. cit., and Schwartz (1985), op. cit., for a discussion of Mozi and the Mohist school of philosophy.

the principle of *ai*. *Ai*, usually translated as "all-embracing love," resembles Confucius's idea of ren. But Mozi thought that ren did not go far enough. Rather than merely refraining from doing things to others that you would not want others to do to you, living according to ai means: "to love all men everywhere alike."[116] As Mozi explains it, in deciding what to do we should give equal consideration to the interests of all persons affected by our action. We should not value the welfare of our neighbors more highly than we value the welfare of strangers, or the welfare of our own family more highly than the welfare of our neighbor's family, or our own personal welfare more highly than anyone else's welfare. In short, we should love everyone as we love ourselves.

Mozi thinks it obvious that we would all be better off if we lived in a society where everyone practiced ai. But what would be best for me is if everyone practiced ai, except me. What I would really like is for everyone else to love me as they love themselves, while I continue to put my own interests first. In that situation, other people will sacrifice their own interests for my benefit, but I will not have to make any sacrifices for them. So, if anyone proposes setting up a society where everyone practices ai, my best option is to pretend to go along, while actually continuing to pursue my own self-interest whenever I can get away with it. Unfortunately for me, I am not the only person smart enough to figure all this out. Other people will reason in the same way: everyone will want to be the only self-interested person in a society of suckers. And, therefore, Master Mo's Utopia will have a hard time getting off the ground.

Of course, the above reasoning holds only if people are purely self-interested. A Confucian might believe that people would be inspired by the moral example of others practicing ai to practice ai themselves. If I have ren, I would not want others to cheat on me, so I would not cheat on them. But Mozi says that this is all wishful thinking. He admits that most people are purely self-interested. Nevertheless, he argues, this fact should not stand in the way of establishing a society based on ai. Ai, he says, is a matter of how people behave, not of how

---

[116] Hughes (1992), op. cit., p. 48.

they feel. The problem is to get people to act in accordance with ai. They can continue feeling just as selfish as they ever did. What we need to do in order to get people to act according to ai is just to fix things so that it is in their self-interest to treat other people as well as they treat themselves. The technique for accomplishing this has already been explained: employ rewards and punishments. Use the two handles to steer people in the direction of ai.

Mozi envisions setting up a hierarchical system. At its head will be a ruler, a "Son of Heaven," with the power to dispense rewards and punishments. This Son of Heaven will decree that those who practice ai will be rewarded and that those who fail to act in accordance with ai will be punished. (Love everybody as you do yourself—or we will cut you in half with a bamboo saw!) If rewards and punishments are distributed efficiently, people will see that it is to their advantage to practice ai. Pursuit of self-interest, guided by the ruler's firm grip on the two handles, will lead people to embrace all embracing love—if not in their hearts, at least in their behavior.

For this system to work, the ruler has to be able to find out who is practicing ai and who is cheating. To get people to do what you want by means of reward and punishment, you must reward those who are actually doing what you want them to do and punish those who are not. So the Son of Heaven will need lots of officials to watch the people and report on their behavior. And, of course, there will have to be officials to watch those officials and so on. "On hearing good or evil, all shall report it to the officers above them, and what they call right, all shall call right: what they call wrong, all shall call wrong."[117]

Here a Confucian might spot a problem in Mozi's system. Recall Confucius's observation that, "If you try to lead people by means of punishments, they will try to avoid them without any conscience"(23).[118] The Son of Heaven's subjects will obey him only because they fear his punishments or hope to secure his rewards. If they can evade these punishments or gain these rewards by deceit,

---

[117] Ibid., p. 66.
[118] Ibid., p. 26.

they will do so. If, for example, I can get away with not practicing ai by bribing my local official to look the other way, I will do so (assuming that I think this to be in my self-interest). Since my local official is also a purely self-interested human being, he will take that bribe, if he can get away with it. At best, Mozi's Son of Heaven is going to need a lot of officials, and a lot of officials will cost a lot of money. At worst, the system will soon be rotten with corruption, the ruler will be unable to get reliable information about who is practicing ai, and the two handles will come off in the ruler's hands as he tries to steer the society toward all-embracing love.

Mozi recognizes this problem, however, and he has a solution to it. The solution lies in religion. Mozi does not plan to rely only on fallible, corruptible human officials to maintain order in his Utopia. The ruler will announce that ai is not just a good idea, it represents the law of heaven. "What standard may be taken as suitable for ruling," Mozi asks? "The answer is that nothing is equal to imitation of Heaven." An what is the standard of heaven? "What does Heaven want and what does it hate? Heaven wants men to love and be profitable to each other, and does not want men to hate and maltreat each other."[119] And heaven will not stand idly by while men violate its law: nor will it allow those who keep its law to go unrewarded. "I say that Heaven is sure to give happiness to those who love and benefit other men, and is sure to bring calamities on those who hate and maltreat other men."[120]

Confronted only by human officials whose knowledge is limited and whose virtue might be for sale, a selfish wrong-doer might hope to avoid the ruler's punishments. But suppose I believe that rewards and punishments are dispensed, not only by human officials, but by a power that knows all that I do and whose punishments I cannot escape. If I am convinced that this power will reward me for practicing ai and rain calamities on me if I fail to live up to that standard, then clearly the rational, self-interested thing for me to do is to become the best exemplar of ai that I can be. Thus, in Mozi's Utopia everyone will

119 Ibid., p. 45.
120 Ibid., p. 46.

be taught that: "Even in the deepest gorges and great forests where there is no man, one may not act improperly. There are ghosts and spirits who will see."[121]

Does Mozi really believe all this stuff about ghosts and spirits punishing evil-doers? Probably so. His book contains several purportedly eyewitness account of the spirits meting out justice to evil-doers.[122] But, that is not the essential point. The point is rather that, if a society wants to maintain order, it is a good idea for it to get people to believe that Heaven will punish wrongdoing. Mozi sees his own society declining into a condition of more disorder. "What are the causes of this decline?" he asks.

> Logically there are doubts as to the difference made by the spirits existing or not existing, and the failure to realize the power of the spirits to reward the worthy and punish the bad. Supposing now that all men believed in the spirits having power so to reward and punish, how could society be in confusion? The people today who deny the existence of spirits . . . cause people to doubt whether [spirits exist]; and this is the way in which society falls into chaos.[123]

By promoting belief in heaven's power to reward and punish, Mozi hopes to convince naturally self-interested people that "there is no safety but in doing good."

With heaven on the side of ai, Mozi thinks that society need not depend on family training or on li to encourage the development of virtue. Indeed, he views both family relationships and li with suspicion. The former can lead to partiality or discrimination in love. We should love our own children no more than we love anyone else's children. We should have no more regard for our own parents, than we have for other people's parents. Ai demands that we love all equally. Li, the rites and ceremonies so valued by Confucius, Mozi dismisses as a waste of time and resources that could be better expended on providing practical benefits to our fellow citizens. Except in so far as

---

[121] Creel (1953), op. cit., p. 61.
[122] See, e.g., Hughes, op. cit., p. 52.
[123] Ibid., p. 51.

rituals might be used to inculcate belief in the power of the spirits to reward and punish, Mozi sees no place for such mumbo-jumbo in his Utopia of all-embracing love.

A CONFUCIAN LOOK AT MOZI'S UTOPIA

One of Confucius's disciples remarks in the *Analects* that, "The Master's views on the fine externals of culture we often have the privilege of hearing, but not his views on . . . the ways of Heaven" (5.12).[124] Modern scholars are uncertain of the exact nature of Confucius's personal religious beliefs. But whatever they may have been, he seldom invokes heaven when discussing politics or morality. He never suggests that heaven will reward those who achieve ren or punish those who fall short of it. Rather, as we have seen, he says that an honorable person cultivates ren, not in the expectation of reward, but because such a person's sense of honor demands it. What would Confucius have to say then about Mozi's plan to use belief in heavenly reward and punishment to enforce individual virtue and social order?[125]

We can be confident that he would not approve of Mozi's attitude toward the family and toward li. Confucius thinks that good behavior arises from good character, that is, one's inner moral power. And he sees good character, not as matter of rational calculation of profit and loss, but as matter of emotion and habit. It is these which are shaped by family life and li into ren. When Mozi devalues family and li, he is, in Confucius's view, undermining the real foundations of moral behavior and social order. Confucius would deny that the fear inspired by threats of punishment or the greed excited by the prospect of reward, could be an adequate substitute for character in shaping human conduct.

Further, a Confucian might well wonder how Mozi proposes to get people to believe in heavenly rewards and punishments, and whether, if he succeeded, these beliefs would have the effects on human behavior that Mozi expects them to have. History is full of societies

---

[124] Ibid., p. 14.
[125] To discover exactly what later Confucians did say about Mozi's ideas, see Graham (1989) and Schwartz (1985), op. cit.

that have expended enormous efforts in order to get people to accept beliefs that are supposed to turn them into loyal, cooperative subjects or citizens. As the recent examples of the former Soviet Union, Eastern Europe, and the People's Republic of China illustrate, such efforts often prove to be spectacularly unsuccessful. Our own society has spent three decades trying to teach people to believe in racial equality. Many find the results of those efforts disappointing.

Why such lack of success? Perhaps, societies often do not succeed in getting people to really believe what the rulers want them to believe. We do not know all that much about how to get large numbers of people to accept a given belief and even less about how people accept a belief that will fundamentally change their lives. If Mozi knew how to do this, it is a pity that he did not tell us. (On second thought, maybe it's a blessing.)

It is also possible that, as Confucius thought, people's beliefs have less influence on their behavior than we might expect. After all, there have been many people who have believed that, if they failed to live the right sort of lives, heaven would punish them, perhaps even punish them eternally. If people's beliefs are what determine their behavior, then those who believe in eternal punishment for sin should find it quite easy to avoid sinning. Whatever pleasures there might be in lust, greed, pride, and all the rest, those pleasures are surely only temporary. If I really believed that my indulgence in such sins would be punished by everlasting torment in hell, and if my beliefs were all that determined my behavior, why should it be difficult for me to avoid sinful behavior? But even people who believe firmly in hell often report that sin remains a constant temptation and that they sometimes fail to resist it. Perhaps, then, belief matters less than we imagine. Perhaps our upbringing, our emotions, our habits have a greater impact on our behavior than do our beliefs.

CONCLUSION

So, were the secularist philosophers of the European Enlightenment correct in thinking that they had found an ally in Confucius? If they were looking for someone who believed that public morality and that social order need not be enforced by threats of divine punishment, then they were right to look to Confucius. To the extent that religion supplies no more than self-interested motives for good behavior, Confucius had little use for religion. In his view, public order arises from the people's confidence in their rulers. Rulers can win this confidence only by cultivating their own moral power and not by frightening people into obedience with tales about the spirits.

But if we think of religion as part of li—as a body of rituals, ceremonies, and practices that draws people together, that shapes habits of "mutual yielding" and respect, that calls forth feelings of awe and gratitude toward the community and the larger world in which we live—then Confucius attaches great importance to religion. He is certainly no ally of those who believe that a successful human society can be founded on reason alone. Partisans of that viewpoint might find a more congenial companion in Mozi.

8
Conclusions and Reflections
▼ ▼ ▼

We have not organized our discussion around a single theme that ties
together the individual chapters and leads the reader toward some
overall conclusion. There is no moral to our story. Instead, each
chapter tells its own story with its own moral. So rather than trying to
sum up everything, we shall conclude with some further reflections
on a few of the ideas introduced in the individual chapters. We shall
collect reflections under the general headings, "Religion and Morality," "Religion and the Meaning of the Universe," and "Religion and
Community." Each topic concerns, in different ways, the connection
between religion and our understanding of our lives in this world.

RELIGION AND MORALITY

Many people see a close connection between religion and morality.
This belief is prevalent in North American society. Panels and com-
missions set up to address moral issues about biomedical research or
housing the homeless generally include members of the clergy and
others with professional training in religion. People troubled by marital difficulties, substance abuse, and other personal problems often
seek advice of religious counselors. Many believe that attending
religious services or exposing children to religious values in education
will improve people's behavior.

We have mentioned several sorts of connections between religion and morality in our previous discussions. Confucius emphasized that religion fosters a sense of community and identification with other persons, which is in turn a precondition of ethical conduct, and Mozi asserted that God enforces the moral law. Historical Judaism defined the moral law in an orthopraxy rather than in an orthodoxy, and used such behavioral norms to define membership in its community. Mohammed curbed the lawlessness of the Arab clans, and stopped the cycles of blood feuds, by imposing a moral law based on Allah's will that also bound the clans together in a wider identity and community as Muslims. Further, our general convictions about the nature of the world in which we live and its relation to the rest of reality must influence our judgments about how we ought to live, and of course, religious beliefs form, for most people, a crucially important part of their general picture of reality. This was the theme of our discussion of Jesus' moral teachings.

But believers often see a deeper, more specific connection between religion and morality. Many people feel that moral values represent an objective, intrinsic feature of reality. They insist that right and wrong, good and evil, are not just matters of human preferences. In their view, slavery, for example, is an unjust practice even if no human beings (not even the slaves themselves) think that it is unjust. Similarly, these people hold that all are bound by the moral law, even if we do not abide by it, or acknowledge its existence. Confucius and various other philosophers, such as the Greek thinker Socrates, believed that we can account for the objective reality of moral values without bringing God into the picture.[126] For many people, however, it is precisely the existence of God that explains the objectivity of the moral law.

One might acknowledge this explanation in a variety of different ways, but perhaps the most common strategy is what is usually called the Divine Command Theory. According to this approach, God does not merely enforce the moral law, God is also the author of the moral laws. God sets up the standard of right and wrong. Human

---

[126] On this question, see Plato's dialogue *Euthyphro* (many translations). A good summary of this point can be found in James Rachels, *The Elements of Moral Philosophy*, 2d ed. (New York: McGraw-Hill, 1993), chap. 4, "Does Morality Depend on Religion?," pp. 44–61.

judgments of right and wrong are either true or false according to whether they agree with the divine standard. Whether a certain sort of human action is morally right, for example, eating pork or having an abortion, depends on whether it is forbidden or permitted by God's commands. Differences of opinion among human beings about the moral value of an action do not compromise the objectivity of the moral law. Even if human beings unanimously approved of the institution of slavery, that would not make slavery just. It is not what we think that counts; is is what God thinks.

Divine Command Theory has a bad name among many contemporary philosophers who contend that, although the theory may make moral values independent of human preferences, it does so by making them dependent on God's arbitrary preferences. If God's commanding something is what makes it right, then, if God had commanded us to commit adultery or murder, such actions would be morally obligatory. Faithful spouses would be perverts and peaceable neighbors ought to be punished for their lack of hostility. In the view of its critics, Divine Command Theory turns God into a despot who issues senseless orders to his slavishly obedient, human subjects.[127]

Defenders of this theory have their replies to such charges, but we shall not pursue this debate here. Instead, we shall be content to observe that, even if one does not think that God's commanding something is what makes it right, one might reasonably take God's command as an objective reference point for evaluating human action. Why? In purely human contexts, we often put our trust in the judgments of those who are wiser and more virtuous than ourselves. Supposing that God is infinitely wise and infinitely good, we have great reason to trust God's judgment rather than our own. Similarly, the fact that an omnipotent, omniscient creator of the universe cares about right and wrong should impress on us the majesty and ultimate significance of moral values. If God respects the moral law, it cannot simply result from human convenience.

Furthermore, Judaism and Christianity stress that, in addition to

---

[127] Bertrand Russell seems to picture God this way in his *Why I Am Not a Christian*. (Simon and Schuster, New York, 1957)

God's omniscience and omnipotence, there is a special relationship between God and the subjects of morality that explains the special obligations of his subjects to obey the moral law. In Judaism, the Jews are special because they are the Chosen People who covenanted with God and who, in turn, are especially bound to uphold the moral law. In Christianity, if we can assume that everyone acknowledges what the moral law is, then explaining why Christians are obligated is straightforward: God cares about each individual and how his or her life goes. Because of such caring, moral rules were bequeathed to humans, which they can choose to follow or not follow. But the rules are for their own good and, ultimately, their own salvation. Christians choose to ignore the advice of such a brilliant, benevolent God only at their great peril.

The above account suggests how religious beliefs can provide support for the idea that moral values are objectively real and ultimately significant. There are ways to attack this argument, for example, by attacking the assumption that to be objective or significant, such values must be anchored in some metaphysical source such as God or the nature of the universe. But we shall not pursue such attacks here, and instead ask whether every religious tradition is so friendly toward the pretensions of morality.

Jesus emphasized that salvation, not the moral perfection of society, is the goal of our human existence. Mohammed largely concurs. Both insist that salvation comes to us, not because we have made ourselves worthy of it, but by God's grace and in spite of our unworthiness. What we absolutely must do to be saved is to submit to God—to throw ourselves on God's infinite mercy. As we saw in chapter 2, wholehearted commitment to salvation might lead us to reject the demands of conventional morality. Even if we think that submission to God requires us to live according to a standard higher than that of conventional morality—not merely to respect our neighbor's rights, but to love our neighbors as ourselves—conformity to that standard still is a means to an end, not the end in itself. Salvation is the end; morality is at most a part of the submission or repentance that brings salvation.

The focus on salvation by God's grace has led some believers to a sort of contempt for morality. The Russian holy man Grigorii Rasputin is said to have believed that attempts to live according to the moral law are evidence of the sin of pride and one's lack of faith in God's mercy. Devotion to the moral law indicates a belief that we can earn salvation by our own efforts (which shows pride) and that God can save us only if we make ourselves worthy (which shows lack of faith). Fortified by this view, Rasputin freely indulged in gluttony, drunkenness, and gross sexual immorality—thus demonstrating both proper Christian humility and complete faith in God's infinite mercy. Though somewhat unconventional, Rasputin's attitude taps into genuine tendencies in Christianity.

Still, one could argue that, even if moral relationships among humans pale in significance when compared to our relationship to God, our relationship to God is a personal relationship, and hence, a moral relationship. God approaches us with love, mercy, and infinite concern; in return, we approach him with gratitude, respect, and devotion. God promises us eternal life under his protection, and we put our trust in his promise. Thus the relationship that is the center of our reality is ultimately a moral relationship.

But, as we saw in chapters 5 and 6, this conception of the ultimate significance of moral values is rejected in the Upanishads and by Buddhism. The distinctions between good and evil, right and wrong, belong strictly to the world of names and forms (together with all other distinctions). They are part of *maya*, that is, of things as they appear to us, not as aspects of Brahman's ultimate reality. When we recognize our oneness with Brahman, we leave good and evil behind:

> He who knows the joy of Brahman ... is free from fear. He is not distressed by the thought, "Why did I not do what is right? Why did I do what is wrong?" He who knows the joy of Brahman, knowing both good and evil, transcends both. (Taittiriya Upanishad)[128]

Moksha liberates us from seeing reality from the moral point of view, just as it frees us from all our other human limitations.

[128] Prabhavandanda and Manchester, op. cit., p. 58.

Buddhism rejects the Upanishadic idea of an underlying, permanent reality and rejects positing the goal of human life as union with this reality. But the Buddhist view of moral values is essentially the same as that of the Upanishads. The Buddha teaches that, to achieve enlightenment, one must "see through" and become indifferent to moral distinctions. Nibbana, like moksha, represents freedom from the limitations of personhood. Concerns about right and wrong are part of those limitations and moral values have no reality except within those limits.

The above contrast may seem to overlook the role of karma, both in the Upanishadic tradition and in Buddhism. Isn't karma a sort of moral law? Are we not punished for our bad deeds and rewarded for our good ones, when we are reborn into a new life? This is indeed how many ordinary Hindus and Buddhists think about karma. They believe that those who are miserable in this life are reaping the consequences of their misdeeds in a previous life. For them, karma represents cosmic justice. Whatever happens to us results from our actions in some previous life.

But there are some important distinctions between the idea of karma that we described in chapters 5 and 6 and the idea of a moral law. First, karmic benefits and misfortunes are simply naturalistic consequences of our actions, not rewards or punishments dispensed by some divine law-enforcement agency. Karma operates almost mechanistically. If you steal a dozen unripe peaches from your neighbor's yard and eat them, you might get a stomachache and you might be arrested and have to pay a fine. The stomachache is a natural consequence of your action, but the fine is a punishment. Karma is more like the stomachache. Reality simply works in such a way that a given action naturally produces a given result. No intelligent intervention by an outside agent is required, and no deliberation is needed about the appropriate punishment or reward.

Further and importantly, the really significant karmic consequence of your actions is not rebirth into this or that particular kind of life, but rebirth itself. The ultimate goal is not to be reborn into a happy life: indeed, both the Upanishads and the Buddha maintain that no human life is really satisfying. The goal for each is to escape from the whole pointless cycle of birth and rebirth. And what leads to that escape is not good deeds as such, but breaking attachments to the things of this world. It is not actions themselves that bind us to the wheel of samsara, but the desires from which actions arise. So any desires for the things of this world bind us to the wheel. Hating your neighbor binds you to the wheel, but so does loving your neighbor.

Does this mean that the Upanishads and the Buddha teach an amoral approach to life? Certainly not in one sense of amoral. Both regard morality as an important facet of life in this world. Both likewise teach we cannot achieve enlightenment without scrupulously avoiding all the conventional forms of human wrongdoing. But neither regards conventional good behavior as anything more than a very preliminary step on the road to liberation. Nor does either find any significance in morality beyond its significance in this world. Both see moral values as a reflection of human desires, not as a revelation of the mind of God, or the Way of Heaven, or of any ultimate reality.

So there is no simple, one-size-fits-all story to tell about the relation between religion and morality throughout all the world's religions. If one gets his religion from the Tanak, the Gospels, or the Koran, one may find a place for moral values in the heart of ultimate reality. But if one takes the Upanishads or Tripitaka as one's guide, one will consign moral values to the world of appearances and to the status of fleeting manifestations of human desire. Similar conclusions can be drawn from the Chinese religious traditions. Mozi will tell you that belief in divine rewards grounds peace in civil society, but Confucius dismisses this belief as both unnecessary and unworthy. Overall, our conclusion here about religion and morality may seem disappointing to some, but it seems to be the only one that does justice to the diversity of the world's religious traditions.

RELIGION AND THE MEANING OF THE UNIVERSE

We expect religious beliefs to be deeply involved in questions about how we ought to live. We would also expect them to be involved in questions about the nature of the world in which we live. This expectation is borne out in contemporary discussions of Creationism and Big Bang cosmology, as well as in numerous references found in historical studies to conflicts between science and religion. Our first chapter explored one instance of such a conflict when it discussed the collision between Greek naturalism and ancient Judaism. Rather than develop further specific contrasts between particular religious worldviews and particular scientific views, we will now concentrate on the big picture.

One of the things that religion is supposed to tell us about the world in which we live is what it all means. Science acquaints us with the facts about how the world is; religion tells us why it is the way it is. It is this idea about the contribution of religion to our understanding of the universe that we want to explore.

Here are two possible views of the universe:

1. The material world in which we currently find ourselves represents only one aspect of a larger reality. Space, time, and the other physical conditions that govern our day-to-day lives are expressions of a deeper, more fundamental realm of existence. This more fundamental reality has shaped the material world and directs it toward certain ends. Nothing in the material world is accidental, nothing is purposeless, once we see things from the perspective of the larger reality.

2. The material world is all the reality there is. Once we have described its basic physical constituents, there is no deeper or more fundamental level to which we can turn for further explanation of the way the world is. No purpose or plan governs the universe. It is governed only by the laws of nature. These laws represent, not directives originating outside the physical universe, but simply regularities or predictable patterns that happen to occur in the universe. They reveal not how things ought to be according to some design, but merely how things are.

We have resisted attaching labels to these worldviews for reasons that will become apparent as we develop our discussion. But the first view is often thought of as a religious view of the universe. It is certainly the view associated with Judaism, Christianity, and Islam. They see God as the most important component of the larger reality in which the physical universe exists. God's intelligence and will supply the meaning of purpose of the universe, and his power shapes the universe to suit his purpose. The second view represents a materialistic account of the universe and is often thought of as the worldview of modern science.

Of course, the association between view 2 and science overlooks the fact that many scientists themselves operate within something more like view 1. Indeed, the so-called religious view of the universe is by no means inimical to the practice of science. View 1 implies that the universe is a rational, orderly place, and a belief to that effect encourages people to think they can discover that order. Further, because the universe is shaped by God even to the smallest detail, it must reveal a good deal about the nature of God. We could learn something about you by studying a building you designed. According to view 1, the universe represents God's handiwork and is thus, potentially, a rich source of information about the mind of God. View 1 provides us, then, with powerful motives for wanting to investigate the physical universe. Regardless of the history of conflicts between particular religious institutions and particular programs of scientific investigation, there is certainly no reason to see the religious outlook itself as an obstacle to the development of natural science.

However, to call view 1 the only religious approach is inaccurate. It represents the approach in some religious traditions, notably Judaism, Christianity, and Islam. The Upanishads present a picture of the world that is just as devoid of meaning and purpose, as that of any scientific worldview. In the Upanishadic conception, Brahman is not an agent. Brahman is without desire and without will. Brahman has no purposes and entertains no plans. The universe represents a manifestation or expression of Brahman's reality, but is in no sense a deliberate or meaningful expression. There is no act of creation and no answer to the question, "Why does the universe exist?" or "Why is the universe as it is?" Thus the belief that the universe exists for some reason, or in order to fulfill some purpose, does not go together with belief in God. Rather, it goes with belief in a certain kind of God: a personal, active, willing God.

The Upanishadic worldview does preserve, however, one important feature of the Western religious picture of reality in view 1. It preserves the view that God transcends the world. The world is not the whole of reality. It is a limited and incomplete manifestation of a deeper, larger reality. The material universe is a part or aspect of Brahman, but Brahman is not the universe. Brahman is something much more, much greater. According to the Upanishads, in order to understand reality and our place in it, we must look beyond the world. When we look beyond the world, we will not discover its meaning or purpose—it has none—but we will discover the ultimate, liberating truth that the world is not all there is. This affirmation of existence of a transcendental reality, a reality beyond the world, is also at the heart of the Western religious tradition.

But even the affirmation of a transcendental reality disappears when we turn to Buddhism. At least in the austere version of the Buddha's teachings, that we explored in chapter 6, the Buddha abandons not only belief in a personal God, but in any reality existing behind or outside of the world or appearance. Of course, in one sense, Buddhism is concerned with going "beyond the world," that is, it is concerned with the problem of how to escape from the world. But this is not escape into another, higher reality. It is rather extinguishing our own involvement with, and ultimately, our presence in, this world. And the key to achieving this escape (nibbana) lies in coming to understand that there is no transcendental reality. Enlightenment consists in seeing the world, not as a manifestation of some underlying reality, but simply as it is, as a ceaseless flow of appearances. And we must also understand that we ourselves are part of this flow of appearances and that we can have no existence outside it. Nibbana comes with the realization that it is only our deluded belief that we can transcend the world that keeps us in the world, and thus, keeps us returning birth after birth to the misery of samsara.

Although Buddhism does not share the materialistic perspective of view 2, it fully endorses view 2's rejection of a reality behind the world as it appears to us. So the conflict between views 1 and 2 is as much a conflict among different religious understandings of the material world as it is a conflict between religion and modern science. Though it is conventional to say that religion provides an explanation of the meaning of the universe, it turns out that in some religions the explanation is that the universe has no meaning. Furthermore, view 2 is not a modern view, distinctively associated with contemporary, Western science, but an ancient view that is just as much a religious outlook as view 1.

RELIGION AND COMMUNITY

Religions thus differ greatly from each other about their most substantial philosophical claims. Such differences make some people despair about religion, and they infer that unless universal agreement can be had, religion is all a hopeless morass. Nevertheless, perhaps the brightest spot about religion concerns its ability to nurture fellow-feeling among its members. We now conclude with a few remarks about how such fellow-feeling grows within religions despite the many philosophical problems within these religions. We begin by reviewing three such problems relevant to our previous discussions in this book.

Both scholars of religion and contemporary believers frequently distinguish between the beliefs of the founders and the beliefs and practices of modern organized religion. Our reflections in this book support this distinction. Jesus' message about the Kingdom of God differs markedly from the beliefs of contemporary Christians, who no longer expect the kingdom within their lifetimes and who act accordingly. The original message of the Buddha did not include instructions to the sanghas (orders of monks) on how to organize the religion founded in his name and, as the stories go, the Buddha even steadfastly refused to answer the question of whether it would be a good thing to have sanghas. Similarly, modern Hindus, Moslems, and Confucians differ significantly with the teachings of the original founders of these religions.

Another discrepancy that we have implied in this book concerns the definition of *religion*. Of course it would be parochial for us to take a Western religion as the paradigm of a true religion and dismiss each Eastern version as a simulacrum. Nevertheless, some interesting contrasts appear. For example, if we claim that a necessary condition of having a religion is a belief in an underlying or transcendent reality beyond the appearances of this world, then Hinduism counts as a religion but Buddhism does not. If we add another condition and claim that a God-as-a-person is necessary, then neither Hinduism nor Buddhism count. However, in this case we have tailored the assumptions so carefully to the three dominant Western religions that we really do seem to be interested only in surveying what people in fact take to be religions and only in puffing up our own as the only true religions.

A third discrepancy we have noted is between the attempt to embed morality and meaning in some transcendent reality and what actually occurs in the various world religions. The attempt to do so seems to be a characteristically Western preoccupation, which the Upanishads and Buddhism regard as something that the enlightened person wants to avoid. In fact, neither morality nor meaning seem to require belief in a theistic God who is claimed to have sent periodic revelations to humans. We might observe that meaning is where you find it, and morality's connection to religion might have more to do with what actually works in a particular religious context than with any necessary belief about its transcendent source.

Despite these discrepancies, we would like to end on a more positive note by observing a few things about religion's ability to provide an identity among its members. Perhaps the hallmark of contemporary religion is its ability to create a sense of fellowship among those who periodically gather together. It is interesting that people reap such benefits today as Presbyterians or Baptists and yet might differ very greatly in their beliefs. Indeed, it is common for those attending such churches to have very little idea at all about the theology of their particular denominations, or even the foundational beliefs of Christianity. Similar claims could be made about modern Jews, Hindus, and Confucians.

Such feelings of community or group identity appear very important to a significant portion of the human population. Thinking about community opens an entirely different way of thinking about religion: not as a set of beliefs about reality, God, or God's relationship with humans, but as a way of people being together. Such a view is religion as seen, not by theologians or philosophers, but by psychologists and sociologists.

Even here, adventuresome philosophers might venture a few remarks. Good psychologists and sociologists, when they study religions, usually suspend doubt about the truth-claims of the religion they are studying. Whether it is an animistic religion in Africa or a Sufi branch of Islam, they say to themselves, "What if I really believed as they did too? How would I feel and act?" In this book, we have similarly avoided the ultimate truth-claims of religions about God's existence, about the superiority of each religion to the others, and about the particular claims of each to an ultimate goal for humans. Instead, we have philosophically asked, "What if we thought as they did and what if we assumed their foundational premises? What dilemmas would we then face?"

What was missing from our subsequent discussion of the dilemmas in the religions was a feeling for the rich, substantial sense of community in which these dilemmas live and even thrive. If we were writing as sociologists of religion, we could discuss the diversity and tolerance that exists within some religious traditions for arguments that attack their essential beliefs: we could enter a yeshiva in Jerusalem and hear orthodox boys mounting arguments for the nonexistence of God or his malevolence toward Jews; we could enter an Indian teahouse and hear materialistic Hindus attacking the devotees of Kali, with everyone afterward smiling and appreciating the subtlety of the arguments; we could enter the business of a rich merchant in Indonesia—the country with the most Moslems of any country in the world—to see how the Islam practiced there seems so sophisticated, so urbane, and so educated as to be almost a different religion than the Shi'a Islam of today's Iran.

But if we had to make some parting remark about religion's ability to nurture community, despite its inheritance of logical dilemmas in

its theology and despite the discrepancies between its modern expression and its founder's intentions, we would observe that in the
1960s, many political pundits predicted that religion had lost its
appeal and would soon die out. Instead, what happened was that
during the past decade, there was a remarkable efflorescence of
religious feeling and belief, not only among North Americans but also
among people around the globe. Whatever the status of its beliefs and
internal dilemmas, religion seems to offer to humans something that
they really need.

What is that? One answer to this question is that religion offers to
people precisely this sense of community; of being together for a
common purpose, of feeling not alone in the universe, of having help
in raising a family and in educating children, and of probing together
that somewhat dangerous ground of group philosophical belief. Our
own discussions have shown how the religious traditions of Judaism
and Confucianism evolved to nurture community and let it thrive.
Islam's and Christianity's institutions and practices likewise created
strong ties of community among their members. Modern Shinto religion in Japan and modern Taoism in China, despite a large proportion
of members who no longer believe much in common about the
deities, still provide their members a sense of group cohesion and
meaning at births, funerals, and public ceremonies.

Religion perhaps works best at creating this sense of community,
and our discussion has shown that it can do so in vastly different ways.
Indeed, it can do so in ways where the ultimate philosophical assumptions of a particular religion often contradict similar claims made by
another religion, and yet where each of the two religions creates
strong feelings of community among its members. Perhaps that is its
true power.

We have been suggesting, then, that religion might be able to
create a sense of community among its members even if we hold in
abeyance its claims to truth about ultimate reality, about the source of
morality, and about human existence. To some extent, contemporary
branches of reform Judaism, progressive Sunni Islam, and liberal
Christianity do just that. Similar claims could be made about Taoism,
Confucianism, Hinduism, Japanese Shinto religion, and Buddhism in

the East. However, there is of course a nagging dilemma here, too, because such claims can only be held in abeyance for so long. Ultimately, if members of a group do not believe the same about reality, do not believe the same about morality or its source, or do not believe the same about God, then one wonders in one sense if they are a real religious community. Ultimately, one wonders whether such communities will continue to exist, for one test of any such community is what beliefs its members are ready to shed blood for. Without some such deep agreement, modern feelings of community might be a mere shell.

We conclude that religion in this world is a mansion with many rooms. Some people need a room marked "Truth;" others just don't want to sleep alone. Some enter and want to go to the archives; others need the infirmary to make it through the night. All the rooms are part of religion, and all, at least, provide a place to sleep.

Index

▼ ▼ ▼

151

Babylonian Talmud, 23
Baptists, 146
Bar Kochba, 21, 23
bastards in Judaism, 4
Bathsheba (Uriah's wife), 3
Battle of the Trench, 61
bhikkus (monks), 102
Bickerman, Elias, 17
Big Bang cosmology, 142
blasphemy, 45
blood feuds (before Mohammed), 62
Bodhi (Bo) tree, 96
body, Jewish attitude to versus Greek,
     10, 11
Book of Documents (and Confucius),
     122
Boswell, John, 11
Brahman, 80
  does not need consciousness, 94
  knowledge of brings freedom from
     fear, 139
  oneness with, 139
  nature of Brahman, 88
  not a person, 91
  not an agent, 91
  likeness to a thing, 94
  ultimately is everything, 89
Branch Davidians, 23
brothels, 11
Buddha
  life, 96ff
  teaches only about suffering and cure
     for it, 102
  view on enlightenment, 105ff
Buddha-Gaya, 96
Buddhism, 146
  Upanishadic system and, 105
  morality and, 140–141
  material world and, 144–145

Caesar, 31
Caligula, 18
caliph, 62
Calvin, John, 73
Canaanites, 69
canonization of the Scriptures, 13
charity
  teachings of Jesus and, 37

teachings of Mohammed and, 62
Chosen People, Jews as, 3, 4, 17, 20, 22
Christology, 50
circumcision, 1, 10, 17
  Paul drops requirement, 47, 55
  of Jewish male babies, 17
citizenship in Greek empires by Jews,
     17
community, 123–124, 136, 145ff
  li and, 124, 134
  religion and, 147
compatiblism, and free will, 72
Confucius
  critics and, 126
  life and, 117ff
  politics and religion and, 114ff
  Mozi's utopia, his view of, 132
consciousness
  Brahman and, 94
Copts, 66
Council of Chalcedon, 66
Council of Jerusalem, 47
Council of Nicea, 66
courage
  ancient Greek military virtue, 9
  whether Jesus on cross exhibits, 53
courts in Judaism, 24
covenant of Jews with YHWH, 2, 17, 18
Creation, 91, 93
Creationism, 142
Cromwell, Oliver, 65

David, King, 3
David Koresh, 23
Day of Judgment, 22
Dead Sea Scrolls, 22
Deborah (general), 69
Descartes, Rene, 54
desire (tanha)
  Brahman and, 90
  Buddhism and, 100–105
  self and, 105–106
  suffering (dukkha) and, 100
  Upanishads account of, 86–87
determinism, 72
devas, 81
devil, 39
dhamma (dharma), 98, 100